BUDDY STALL'S
NEW ORLEANS

BUDDY STALL'S
NEW ORLEANS

by GASPAR J. ("BUDDY") STALL

PELICAN PUBLISHING COMPANY
GRETNA 1990

Library of Congress Cataloging-in-Publication Data

Stall, Gaspar.
 Buddy Stall's New Orleans / by Gaspar J. ("Buddy") Stall.
 p. cm.
 ISBN 0-88289-813-2
 1. New Orleans (La.)—History—Miscellanea. I. Title.
 F379.N557S73 1990
 976.3'35—dc20 90-40789
 CIP

Illustrations by Lane Casteix

Manufactured in the United States of America
Published by Pelican Publishing Company, Inc.
1101 Monroe Street, Gretna, Louisiana 70053

*This book is dedicated
to my four greatest achievements:
Peggy, Gary, Kirt, and Laurie,
my children.*

*They in turn have given
my wife and me untold hours
of happiness, joy, and pride,
not to mention
nine beautiful grandchildren.*

Contents

Acknowledgments

Special thanks to Carol Rohde, Clyde Morrison, Lane Casteix, Frank Stewart, and Henry Gondolfo, as well as to the following people:

Beau Bassich and his City Park staff
Mrs. Harriet Callahan, Louisiana State Library
Mr. Collier Hammer and the entire staff of the Louisiana Division, New Orleans Public Library
Pamela Arceneaux and the entire staff of the Historic New Orleans Collection

BUDDY STALL'S
NEW ORLEANS

CHAPTER 1

Men Who Left Their Marks

John Law
Oliver Pollock
Angelo Secola
Commander Howard W. Gilmore
Ernest "Sunshine Sammy" Morrison
Louis Moreau Gottschalk
Dr. Charles Edmund Kells
Robert Charles
Isaac Monroe Cline
Bernard Mandeville Marigny

John Law (The New Orleans Book, *1915)*

JOHN LAW

John Law was a most unusual Scotsman. He was unusual in that he believed wholeheartedly in the phrase "Laissez Les Bon Temps Rouler." His philosophy was that if you earn a hundred dollars today, spend it today, for tomorrow may never come.

Law was a mathematical genius, adventurous speculator, and a confirmed gambling addict. When his gambling pursuits didn't go well, he simply lived with and was supported by other men's wives (Lake Catherine was named for one of those good ladies) while the husbands were busy earning their fortunes.

During one of these escapades, he learned from a banker's wife he was living with about the Egyptian and Chinese use of paper money in banking operations. He worked hard and sold the old idea of banking with paper money to the Duke of Orleans, who was then serving as the regent of France, as the king was a small child. The Duke was thrilled with the idea of receiving gold and silver and issuing paper money in return. The banking operation was to be called "The Company of the West"—later "The Company of the Indies."

Those who invested their gold and silver in The Company of the West would receive royalties from the tariffs collected at the new port city which was to be built on the Mississippi River. The new city was to be called "New Orleans" in honor of the Duke of Orleans.

Law did a fantastic job of promoting the new venture. He had a colorful poster distributed throughout Europe showing the horn of plenty represented as a great river whose banks were rich with exotic food, precious metals, ample supplies of fresh water, and, of course, beautiful maidens. The financial results were phenomenal, with those investing in the banking venture earning substantial gains from their investments.

Unfortunately, the Duke of Orleans proved to be a greedy man and forced Law to print more and more paper money until the bubble burst and inflation was born. John Law is known in history, not as the man responsible for the city of New Orleans, but as the father of inflation.

OLIVER POLLOCK

If you were to ask a hundred dyed-in-the wool true-blooded (New Orleanian) Americans who Oliver Pollock was, chances are they would answer in unison, "Oliver who?" Yet his $370,000 contribution to the American cause of freedom was the single largest financial contribution received by the desperate Americans.

He was a super-duper salesman, and with 300 to 400 boats trading on the rivers of North America, plus ships traveling to every major port in the world, he was one of the wealthiest men in North America.

Pollock freely gave not only money but much-needed supplies to the Americans during the revolution. Besides his financial support, he used his remarkable salesmanship to convince the Spanish, under the able leadership of Governor Galvez, to aid the American cause by driving the English out of Baton Rouge, Natchez, Mobile, and Pensacola.

When Pollock's finances ran out, he pledged his credit to the limit with the Spanish authorities in order to furnish the Americans additional urgently needed supplies. When the fighting was over and freedom secured, Pollock hurried to Congress in Philadelphia for some assistance, with his creditors hot on his heels. He received a very cool reception from Congress. They too, no doubt, said, "Oliver who?"

To improve his financial situation, he went on a business trip to Cuba, where he was instantly thrown into jail for eighteen months by the Spanish authorities. Luckily, his

old friend, Galvez, found out about his situation and bailed him out to the tune of $151,693. Pollock made a gentleman's agreement to pay the sum back. He also convinced one of his loyal employees to stay in jail in his place until he paid the sum (we said he was a super salesman), which he did.

In spite of the shabby treatment he received from Congress, on October 10, 1786, ten years after America's independence, he was proud to stand and receive his American citizenship.

It just seems that the American government, for one reason or another, had it in for Oliver Pollock, as he has received very little recognition in our history books, and the only two portraits ever painted of him were destroyed during the Civil War by the United States federal gunboat *Essex*.

Today, the only physical reminders of the great man from New Orleans, who did so much to help the Americans win their freedom, are a plaque in the 400 block of Chartres Street, where he once lived, and a town in central Louisiana named in his honor.

ANGELO SECOLA

We all know that one of the main staples of the Louisiana diet is rice. We consume it in enormous quantities and in every imaginable way, from plain rice with butter to the fancy jambalaya and gumbo dishes to a dessert called rice pudding.

But the popularity of rice in Louisiana was not always that great. In fact, as late as the 1840s, only 20,000 sacks of rice per year were harvested in Louisiana, and only in Plaquemines Parish.

That all changed with the arrival in 1849 of an 18-year-old Italian immigrant with a deep desire to make his mark and a contribution to his newly-adopted country.

ANGELO SECOLA
1,000,000 SACKS PER YEAR

His first task was to learn the English language. He had very little trouble, as he already spoke six different languages. His next task was to find employment. Again, no problem. He took a job with A. Gondolfo Import/Export Co., and in just 10 years, he owned the company.

In his travels around Louisiana, he saw vast acres of reasonably priced lowlands not being used. He decided to dedicate himself to producing enormous quantities of rice, as well as to his number one dream, which was to produce the finest quality of rice ever conceived of by man.

Again, with very little trouble he succeeded. Productivity in Louisiana rose to over one million sacks per year of the highest-quality rice in the entire world.

He was also a humanitarian, for he shared his valuable knowledge with the underprivileged countries of the world, and was awarded gold medals by all of the grateful countries that he helped.

The next time you eat a plate of red beans and rice or throw a handful of rice at a wedding, please remember Angelo Secola, the father of the Louisiana rice industry.

COMMANDER HOWARD W. GILMORE

Annapolis graduate Howard W. Gilmore lived at 5315 South Liberty Street in New Orleans.

Those who knew Commander Gilmore describe him as a quiet, mild-mannered man who functioned extremely well under pressure, and a man that was quick to make major decisions without becoming upset by the circumstances which forced them.

During World War II, Gilmore was in charge of the submarine named *Growler*, and under his capable command, growl she did. His efforts in sinking numerous Japanese merchant and war ships, totaling 26,000 tons, led to his receiving the Navy Cross and a gold star in lieu of a second Navy Cross. The circumstances leading to the latter were as follows:

On February 7, 1943, while on patrol in the Pacific, the *Growler*, in order to recharge its batteries, was on the surface. A Japanese gunboat tried to ram the *Growler*, but Gilmore was able to evade the gunboat's rush. The commander maneuvered his awkward pigboat like a skillful yachtsman and sent it crashing at 17 knots into the flank of the Japanese gunboat.

The Japanese ship was done for, but struck back like a venomous snake thrashing in its death throes. The enemy manned heavy machine guns and opened fire; the bullets cut white spray into the blue surface of the water. The lines crept closer to the dark hull of the pigboat. The lead slammed into the steel hull and bridge.

Commander Gilmore calmly gave the first order. "Clear the bridge."

Ratings and officers piled over the protective curtain and into the open hatch of the conning tower in order of rank—the lower the rank, the sooner to reach security. It is navy tradition that the highest officer is the last to seek safety.

The commander waited his turn. The bullets ricocheted and punctured the steel bridge. Several thudded into the body of the commander. He fell.

The men came climbing out of the hatch to pick him up. On the deck of the sinking Japanese gunboat, the crew was working desperately to bring a 3-incher to bear on the sub. The commander gave a second order. "All hands below."

The order was obeyed; it had to be obeyed. Only the officer of the deck remained topside, struggling to lift his fallen commander. The distance between the sub and the enemy gunboat was decreasing. In another moment, the heavy cannon would have a clear shot at the sub. The wounded skipper gave a third and last command. "Take her down."

The deck officer scrambled down the conning tower. The hatch cover slammed shut with an iron clang. As the *Growler* sank into the sea, a projectile from the 3-incher exploded close to the submerging ship but did no damage. Only the top of the conning tower was visible now, the wounded officer still clinging to it.

In a swirl of white salt foam, the submarine vanished beneath the surface. The commander died alone in the sea. Many weeks later, the *Growler*, because of the heroics of its unselfish captain, returned home safely.

Today, midshipmen wandering through Memorial Hall at Annapolis, where the secret relics of the Navy are kept, will see the inscriptions of great fighting men of the sea.

John Paul Jones: "I have not yet begun to fight."
James Lawrence: "Don't give up the ship."

In time we hope they will see:

Commander Howard W. Gilmore: "Take her down."

ERNEST ("SUNSHINE SAMMY") MORRISON

New Orleanian Ernest Morrison was born on December 12, 1912. His father was an outstanding New Orleans chef hired by a family who took him and Sammy to Los Angeles. The move to L.A. proved to be profitable for both Mr. Morrison and his young son, who soon became known as "Sunshine Sammy" because he smiled all the time.

Mr. Hal Roach, silent movie producer of comedy skits with such greats as Harold Lloyd and others, met Sammy and was truly amazed at how fast the young boy learned. Roach was determined to make movies only with children, and the final outcome of that was the successful "Our Gang" comedy series. Sunshine Sammy was considered by some to be the inspiration for the "Our Gang" series. He was the first member of the gang to be hired and was used to work with all the other children during their auditions. He was featured in the original "Buckwheat" role in

twenty-one silent episodes of "Our Gang" comedies before he left the group in 1924.

The young Morrison, under the management of his father, made an extensive personal appearance tour. His father, who proved to be a highly skilled manager, was successful in negotiating a 60 percent share of the gross receipts in some of the appearances, while Sunshine Sammy used his magnetic charm and infectious smile to pack the houses. By age fifteen, Sunshine Sammy had produced his own vaudeville act, billed as—what else—"Sunshine Sammy, the Sepia Star of Our Gang Comedies." Later, he founded the eight-piece band called "Sunshine Sammy and His Hollywood Syncopaters."

By the 1940s, he was back in the movies and every bit as popular as a member of the East Side Kids. In the mid-1950s, with approximately forty years in show business under his belt (or should we say money belt), he took a job in the aerospace industry. He held this job for twenty-seven years. During all of those years, almost none of his co-workers or members of the lodge that he belonged to knew about his show business background until someone caught a glimpse of him on TV at the 1984 Oscars, where Hal Roach received a special Oscar at the Academy Awards Ceremonies.

In 1984, during an interview, and yes, still smiling, Sunshine Sammy told the interviewer, "I was the first black contract player in the movies, the first movie personality to be featured in fan magazines, and the first black to be a millionaire because of the movies. I have good health, drive a Continental Mark IV, and I fall asleep every night counting my many, many blessings."

Sammy's father also collected a first. His chain of grocery stores and wholesale candy firms were the first such black-owned businesses in California.

My name is Louis Moreau
Gottschalk of New Orleans, La.
United States of America

HE IS A ZOMBIE!

HE IS A GENIUS!

LOUIS MOREAU GOTTSCHALK

On May 8, 1829, a son was born to Mr. and Mrs. Edward Gottschalk of New Orleans. It was not known at the time, but this small and seemingly insignificant infant was destined for greatness. In time, he would be known throughout the world, not only by name, but by the unique and haunting compositions he wrote and played.

Each weekend, as a small child, Louis would sit on his porch across from Congo Square, listen to the rhythmic music of the African drums, and watch the slaves dance. These sounds, unbeknownst to him, were later to be used in his compositions.

When only six, he heard his mother, an accomplished pianist, play a new composition she had just received. Upon completion of the piece, she left the room. Louis immediately sat on the piano bench; he was so small his legs did not reach the floor. Having never heard the song before in his life, and not knowing how to read music, he flawlessly played the composition his mother had just completed.

His mother ran back into the room to find out who was playing so beautifully. She was astonished to see her small son at the piano. She said, "He is a genius." The servants whispered as they looked on in shock, "He is a zombie." Child prodigy would have been the proper description. With coaching, his playing accelerated like a runaway train. By the age of seven, he was the organist at St. Louis Cathedral's Sunday morning mass. Before he reached his teens, he was more advanced than even his teachers. It was recommended by one of his instructors that he be sent to Europe to enhance his studies.

At the tender age of thirteen, he applied at the most prestigious school of music in the world, the Paris Conservatory of Music. He was refused without even an audition by the headmaster, Mr. Zimmer. Zimmer considered all Americans barbarians who he claimed made locomotives, not music. Just ten years later, at the same conservatory where he was rejected because of being an American, Gottschalk became the youngest judge ever to serve.

At age fifteen, he held his first performance in Paris at the Salle Pleyel. In attendance was none other than the immortal Chopin. When Gottschalk finished playing, Chopin rose from his seat and said to Gottschalk, "I predict you will become the king of pianists."

Chopin was 100 percent correct. Like fine wine, Louis also got better with age. In his lifetime, he wrote over 100 compositions. The sounds he heard as a child from his front steps across from Congo Square were evident in his compositions, a good example being "Bamboula, Ballade Creole."

Liberace may have taken a few ideas from Gottschalk. Gottschalk was a flamboyant dresser and a magnificent showman who had maiden hearts all over the world beating to his rhythmic, unique style of music. His promotional

talents in the field of music were as great as anyone who ever entered the field. One of his performances he billed as a "Monster Concert." On stage during the performance were 650 musicians and singers. The music that was played and sung onstage was accompanied offstage by cannon fire.

Gottschalk's concerts were in demand throughout the world. He was such a hot commodity, the great P. T. Barnum, considered by most to be the greatest promoter in the world in his day, tried his best to get Gottschalk to sign a contract that would have guaranteed him wealth above and beyond that of anyone who ever played the piano.

But Gottschalk refused. In his own mind, he considered himself, in the musical field, every bit as good a promoter as the great Barnum. He no doubt was, considering that he was able to play where he wanted, when he wanted, and received large sums of money for doing what he loved most. Gottschalk toured Europe, South America, Central America, the West Indies, and every other corner of the world. In between overseas tours he would return to his native land. He played not only in large cities in the U.S., but in remote mining towns as well.

In his day, Gottschalk was the number one musical attraction in the world. People wished to hear him play, and he loved to oblige them. His schedule was horrendous. During the winter of 1855–56, for example, he gave over eighty concerts.

Louis Moreau Gottschalk died on December 18, 1869, while on concert tour in Rio de Janeiro. He was, as Chopin predicted, the king of pianists in his lifetime, as well as America's first musical ambassador.

Being proud of his hometown and country, Gottschalk apparently never forgot being snubbed by the Paris Conservatory of Music. Wherever he went to play, he would always introduce himself as Louis Moreau Gottschalk of New Orleans, Louisiana, United States of America.

DR. CHARLES EDMUND KELLS

C. E. Kells, affectionately called "Eddie" by his friends, was the son of a prominent New Orleans dentist. He began his dental studies at the New Orleans Dental College and graduated from the prestigious New York College of Dentistry in 1878. Upon graduation, as expected, he went into practice with his father. Eddie not only followed in his father's footsteps in the dental field, he was a pioneer trail blazer, and ultimately a martyr, in his chosen profession. It did not take long for him to realize that far too many teeth were being extracted while they were in usable condition. He was very much outspoken in reference to what he considered unnecessary extractions, and is considered one of the profession's earliest preservationists.

Upon learning of the discovery of X-rays in 1896, he immediately began experimenting with this new technique in the field of dentistry. He built an elaborate laboratory in his attic where he spent untold hours. In July 1896, Dr. C. E. Kells became the first man in the world to hold a dental clinic (held in Asheville, N.C.) using an X-ray machine. The auditorium was filled to capacity with those interested in witnessing this new and revolutionary procedure. Because of this demonstration, a female patient eventually lost 50 percent of her hair. Fortunately for her, it did grow back.

What Dr. Kells did not know, nor did anyone else, for that matter, were the devastating effects x-rays would have on his unprotected hands that held the x-ray tube. After administering countless x-rays, the radiation began to take its toll. Dr. Kells lost one finger on his left hand, then a second, shortly after a third, until finally his entire hand and ultimately his left arm were amputated.

This was, it goes without saying, a tremendous loss, but it didn't dampen his spirits or force him to discontinue the practice of dentistry. He was far from ready to throw in the

DR KELLS — 1896— FIRST MAN
IN THE WORLD TO HOLD A DENTAL
CLINIC USING AN X-RAY MACHINE

towel. Instead, he designed special dental tools he could operate with one hand. Over the years, little by little the right hand became affected. In spite of agonizing pain, 42 operations, and numerous skin grafts, his 20-year battle against the ill effects of the exposure to dental x-rays was about to come to an end.

One of Dr. Charles Edmund Kells's favorite quotations went thusly:

> If today seems kind of gloomy
> And your chances kind of slim,
> And the situation's puzzlin'
> And the prospect awful grim,
> Just bristle up and grit your teeth,
> And keep on keepin' on.

When advised by his doctor that his heart and lungs were affected and the end was near—with no left hand or arm, very little of his right hand remaining, and his heart and lungs about to go—there was literally nothing left for him to keep on keepin' on with. On May 7, 1928, in the quiet of his office, where he did so much to aid the field of dentistry, even though he could hardly hold a gun with what little was left of his right hand, he ended his life with a gunshot.

Multitalented

In his lifetime, Dr. Kells received over 30 patents. Not only did he invent instruments for the medical field, such as a suction device used by dentists as well as surgeons, he also invented brakes used in elevators all over the world, fire extinguishers, burglar alarms, and electric door openers, to mention just a few.

A Fighter

When natural gas was introduced in New Orleans he was the first person in the city to cook with gas. The New Orleans Gas & Light Company sued him for using it for cooking, claiming they sold it for lighting purposes only. Dr. Kells was not a man to fool around with when he felt he was right. He brought them to court and, of course, they lost the case.

FIRST PERSON IN N.O. TO COOK WITH GAS!

True Gentleman

Dr. Kells was a shining example of what a gentleman should be. When in an elevator, if a lady entered, he would put down his briefcase (only had one arm) and remove his hat, thereby acknowledging the presence of a lady.

Believer in Equal Rights

Even though others in his profession refused to hire females as assistants, Dr. Kells began the practice of hiring females.

Unique

Dr. C. E. Kells was a unique man in many ways. One way he stood apart from almost every other person was the fact that his body could not tolerate water. If he drank water he would go into convulsions within a very short time. His liquid intake consisted of juices, milk and sherry wine.

ROBERT CHARLES

New Orleans, from its earliest days, has been inhabited by almost equal percentages of white and black citizens. Few other cities can boast of a record with so little animosity or friction between the races. The third week of July, 1900, was an exception. To understand what happened, and possibly why it occurred, we must examine the conditions in New Orleans at the time, as well as happenings in the life of the principal individual in the incident, a black man named Robert Charles.

Robert Charles was born in Copiah, Mississippi in 1865. His parents were still slaves when he was born. When the Civil War ended, of course, slaves were given their freedom. Charles found freedom to be in name only. Many atrocities were inflicted on blacks who had the audacity to vote. He vividly remembered, as a young boy, a black man who received two blasts from a sawed-off shotgun at close range upon casting his ballot. The future of a black man who simply raised his voice, let alone his hand, against a white man was uncertain.

The year 1900, in an economic sense, was a bummer in New Orleans. Unemployment was extremely high, and there were few government programs to help. This factor alone had put a tremendous strain on race relations. With the economy being what it was, white and black citizens were vying for the few jobs that were available. Those who lost out had plenty of idle time to pass.

In the year 1900, Robert Charles had been living in New Orleans for six years. Charles became heavily involved in an organization called the International Migration Society. Their main goal was the return to Africa of all blacks in the United States. Before coming to New Orleans, his only incident involving the police was firing at two white men who were firing at him when he tried to retrieve a stolen gun. In his six years in New Orleans, he had not been

Robert Charles

involved in any recorded incident. This was to change and change drastically.

On Monday, July 23rd, he and a friend went to meet two young women at 2845 Dryades Street. They were to arrive later that evening by train from Baton Rouge. At 11:00 P.M., as the two men sat on the front steps at 2815 Dryades Street (home of white citizens), three officers approached. This innocent confrontation was the beginning of the bloodiest, most anarchic week in New Orleans' history.

When questioned by the police, Charles gave a vague answer. As he stood up, one officer grabbed him and began hitting him with his billy club. Charles pulled away and ran. The officers pulled their pistols and began firing. One bullet struck him in the leg. In the heat of the moment, Charles pulled out his revolver and returned fire, hitting one of the officers.

In spite of his wound, Robert Charles escaped to his home at 2023 Fourth Street. There he attended to his wounds and obtained his rifle. Before he was able to leave, a loud knock sounded on the door. Captain John T. Day, one of New Orleans' most popular and respected officers, backed by numerous policemen, shouted, "Open up there!"

The door slowly opened. Charles quickly stuck the barrel of his rifle close to Day's chest and fired. The bullet went through his heart. Day fell to the ground dead. The other officers were totally surprised and did not return fire. Charles then shot a second officer through the head, killing him instantly. The other officers retreated from the area. From a distance they opened fire, but Charles was able to escape once again.

When the police finally got into RC's room, cocaine, plus evidence that showed his intention was one of harm towards the white race, were found. Word of the murders and evidence collected in the room spread quickly to the people of New Orleans. All hell was ready to break loose. Mobs gathered in the streets and went through the city like the plague, attacking any and all members of the black race. Many wounded and dead lay in their wake. The mayor called out the state militia. He also deputized 500 special police, yet violence continued. The mayor, without hesitation, quickly deputized another 1,000 men. Even with this large number it took several days to bring tranquility back from anarchy.

Through all of the confusion, Robert Charles miraculously made his escape to 1208 South Saratoga Street. Here he spent his time making ammunition for his rifle and administering to his wound. After numerous false sighting reports, on the morning of Friday, July 27th, a police informant advised the chief of police that Charles was in the square of ground bounded by South Saratoga, South Rampart, Clio and Erato Streets.

Sergeant Porteous and three officers were immediately dispatched to the area to search for Charles. Sergeant Porteous, like Captain Day, was shot at close range through the heart and killed instantly. A second officer was shot at the same time. He also died.

Like wildfire, word of the latest encounter spread. In a short time, the block was surrounded by the state militia,

1,500 special deputies, and thousands of other citizens, all carrying guns. It was estimated that over 5,000 armed men surrounded the block.

After shooting and killing the two officers, Charles made his way to the second floor of the building. From a window he shot and killed a civilian in the crowd. He moved from one room to another, firing at will. His accuracy under heavy return fire was unbelievable. He shot twenty more under these adverse conditions. Consideration was given to burning him out; the request was denied. The state militia asked for permission to use the Gatling guns. Permission again was denied.

It was finally decided that he could be safely smoked out by setting a mattress on fire below him, then putting it out and letting the smoke rise to the second floor. This was done. In spite of thick, choking smoke, Charles was able to hold out for twenty more minutes. The smoldering mattress once again caught fire and in turn caught the building on fire.

The only possible escape was down the stairway. When he ran down the stairs he was shot and killed by Charles A. Noret, one of the civilians who had been deputized. As he lay on the ground, Noret shot him three more times. As each man ran into the area, they in turn fired into his body. His body was dragged out in the street in front of 1208 South Saratoga. Many more shots were pumped into his lifeless body.

The crowd started to chant in unison, "Burn him, burn him!" The police acted without hesitation, placing the bullet-riddled body into a police paddy wagon. At a reckless speed, the horse-drawn wagon headed back to police headquarters. Although dead, Robert Charles's head bounced up and down as though he were still alive. The wagon was chased by the mob. They waved their guns and continued to chant, "Burn him, burn him!"

On Sunday morning, July 29th, it was feared that the crowd would turn once again into a mob. To defuse the volatile situation, his body was taken immediately to Potter's Field (Holt Cemetery) and buried in an unmarked grave.

Between Monday, July 23rd, when Charles was approached by police officers, and Sunday, July 29th, when he was buried, he had killed seven white men, including six New Orleans policemen, and wounded twenty others.

The riots of the week of July 23rd were the darkest days ever in New Orleans' race relations.

The *Picayune* newspaper conceded that Robert Charles was an extraordinarily brave and ferociously determined man, but suggested that his deeds were simply the exception which proved the rule that virtually all Negroes were cowards who could never match the fighting ability of the white race. Needless to say, it appears that newspapers at that time did little to foster peace between the races.

ISAAC MONROE CLINE

In 1927, one of the greatest natural disasters in the history of the United States occurred. Heavy snows the previous winter, coupled with heavy rainfall, caused the

mighty Mississippi River to reach a height never before recorded. Flooding up and down the Mississippi River rendered 700,000 people homeless and over $200 million in damages. In Louisiana alone 1,300,000 acres of prime farmland were under water.

New Orleans, a city located in an area below sea level, was very fortunate. Local meteorologist Isaac Monroe Cline, after studying his calculations, advised the city fathers that unless the levees were raised, New Orleans would suffer a major flood. The city heeded his warning by using sandbags to raise the levees, but even with the increased levee height, a small amount of water still lapped over the top.

As the old adage goes, if anything else can go wrong, it usually will. On April 15, 1927, New Orleans recorded its heaviest rainfall in history; in a 24-hour period, the city received 14.94 inches of rain. The coup de grace was the New Orleans Public Service losing all power. The situation was helter skelter. An emergency meeting was called.

After a long conference between the state and city authorities and the U.S. Army Corp of Engineers, it was agreed that the desperate situation in New Orleans required drastic actions. It was feared that the levee might fail from the pressure exerted by the rain and weakened levee conditions. If this happened, there was a good chance that of the 600,000 people who lived in New Orleans, tens of thousands would drown.

It was decided that an artificial crevasse (break in the levee) would have to be made below New Orleans to reduce the level of the flood waters. The logical location decided upon by those in charge was at Caernarvon (13.7 miles below New Orleans), which is located in a sharp bend in the river between the Poydras and Orange Grove plantations.

On April 25, a large crowd gathered on the levee at Caernarvon. Their numbers included engineers, government officials, reporters, and some very irate people whose homes and land would soon be under water. In a sense they were the sacrificial lambs that were to be offered up to save the people of New Orleans.

The people of Caernarvon and the surrounding area were as mad as hornets whose nest had been disturbed. They shouted in unison, "Let Nature take her course and choose her own victims." In response, they were told not to worry, they would all be reimbursed for their losses. This did about as much good calming their anxieties as putting a bandaid on a gunshot wound.

Without delay, divers were sent into the muddy waters to strategically place, well below the water line, 15,000 pounds of dynamite. When all was ready, the crowd was warned to get back and cover their ears to protect themselves from the expected deafening explosion. There was some embarrassment when the demolition superintendent set off the charge and only a soft, muffled sound was heard, doing only enough damage to allow a small trickle through a very small opening.

Over the next two days, divers placed additional tons of dynamite. As each charge was set off, engineers were surprised at just how strong the levees were. One said, "It is almost as difficult to destroy them as it was to build them." After numerous attempts, the crevasse finally opened to 2,600 feet. The waters flowed out of the river, into Breton Sound. As expected, the water level at New Orleans was reduced.

Unexpected was the extremely hostile reaction of those whose homes were sacrificed. Retaliation was expected from the group of home owners on the levee that had little by little transformed into a mob. The National Guard had to be called out. Soldiers with rifles and machine guns were stationed up and down the levees, both above New Orleans and within the city limits, to be sure that none of the threats to blow up the New Orleans levees were carried out.

The one good thing that did come out of the great flood of 1927 was the government's passage in 1928 of an act marking the end of serious flooding in the lower Mississippi Valley. The Bonnet Carré spillway was built, and, when necessary, has been successfully used to divert 250,000 cubic feet of water a second from the Mississippi River into Lake Pontchartrain.

It is interesting to note that John McDonogh, one of the largest landowners in Louisiana in the first half of the 1800's, proposed that a spillway be built at the site of the Bonnet Carré Plantation, the exact location where the government built the Bonnet Carré spillway almost 100 years later.

BERNARD MANDEVILLE MARIGNY

Of all the colorful characters that have called New Orleans home, Bernard Mandeville Marigny has to be close to, if not on, the very top of the list. Bernard's father died,

Bernard Mandeville Marigny

leaving him millions of dollars, while he was still in his teens. With this vast wealth at such a young age, he naturally became very spoiled and uncontrollable. His guardian and uncle, Chalmette, could do little to temper him, so he shipped him off to Paris to be educated, and, of course, at the same time to get him out of his hair.

When Bernard returned, one of the few things he had learned, as well as become addicted to, was a game of chance called "Hazards." The game consisted of two small cubes with one to six dots on each of the six sides. The game was so dangerous to play that the name "Hazards" fit it to a tee.

Bernard so loved the game that once he started playing he would not even stop to eat. Like most Frenchmen, Bernard loved frog legs (*crapaud* in French) and ate them as he played. The Americans, when looking for Bernard to play, would inquire as to the whereabouts of "Johnny Craps" (corruption of the word crapaud). The name of the game called "Hazards," through the corruption of the word *crapaud*, was changed to "craps."

In Bernard's case, Hazards was a more descriptive name for the game. Even though he was a millionaire while still in his teens, he was such a poor player he died penniless. The game he so loved and introduced to North America truly proved to be a "hazard" to his financial well-being.

CHAPTER 2

Truth or Myth?

Was There Ever a Canal on Canal Street?

Did a Meteorite Fall in Audubon Park?

The U.S. Customhouse—Built on a Foundation of Cotton Bales?

You Shouldn't Eat Oysters During Months Without an "R"

Is Spanish Moss a Parasite?

There Is No Mystery Monument!

First Mardi Gras Parade in the U.S.—New Orleans, Louisiana, or Mobile, Alabama?

The Ozone Belt, Supposedly North of Lake Pontchartrain, Is a Figment of Man's Fertile Imagination

There Is No Saint Expedite

WAS THERE EVER A CANAL ON CANAL STREET?

Almost, but not quite.

Once the transfer of the Louisiana Purchase was signed at the Cabildo on December 20, 1803, the population of New Orleans began to soar, as boatload after boatload of new arrivals entered the city. Creoles were not very fond of Americans, and let it be known in no uncertain terms. A wide expanse of land was purposely left between the Creoles and the new arrivals. The area was called "neutral ground," meaning if a Creole or American crossed this area, they were subject to physical harm.

As the American population grew, a serious problem raised its ugly head. Since the mouth of the river was closed to ship traffic more than it was open, due to sandbars, Spanish Governor Carondelet had a canal dug, extending Bayou St. John down present-day Orleans Avenue. At the very end, they installed a turning basin, so that the sailing vessels could turn around to go back to the lake (this is now aptly called Basin Street).

This new canal carried the name Carondelet in honor of the governor who had it dug. The new waterway allowed the Creoles to bring in freight and, more importantly, food products, in a sense right to their doorsteps. The Americans did not have this luxury, in fact, it was a serious problem since they didn't dare cross the neutral ground to use the Carondelet Canal. Plus, between the American section of town and Lake Pontchartrain, there were no roads because of the marshes, prairies, and swamps.

A delegation from the Louisiana territory was sent to Washington with the hopes of having a canal dug from the lake to the edge of the American section of New Orleans. In looking over the situation, Congress decided it would be extremely costly to dig such a canal. Instead, they passed an act on March 3, 1807, authorizing an extension of the Carondelet Canal from the turning basin down present-

PROPOSED CANAL —NEVER BUILT — MAY 30, 1725

day Basin Street. At the neutral ground area, the canal would make a left-hand turn and extend to the Mississippi River. The canal was to be 50 feet wide with a service road on each side measuring 60¼ feet, totalling 170 feet, 6 inches from property line to property line.

The Orleans Navigational Company, empowered by Congress to dig the canal, has a curious place in New Orleans history. They never turned one spade of earth to dig the proposed canal (it was said the Irish contractor ran off to South America with all of the money). The canal never came any closer to reality than a legend on maps of New Orleans. The land in question was reserved for a canal until 1852 by no less an authority than the Congress of the United States. That year, the Orleans Navigational Company became insolvent, and their charter became forfeit. Canal Street was then legally entitled to remain a street 171½ feet wide unless another act of Congress is passed.

It is ironic that the city of New Orleans, with eighty-seven miles of open canals—not counting the granddaddy, the mighty Mississippi River—plus eighty-five miles of canals that are covered over, has a street named Canal that takes its name from a proposed canal that never came to be.

DID A METEORITE FALL
IN AUDUBON PARK?

Nope!

This hoax, still very much believed by many New Orleanians, can be credited to the fertile and mischievous mind of a *Times-Picayune* reporter in 1891. The headline of the newspaper read in bold print "A CELESTIAL VISITOR." The article accompanying the eye-catching headline, which appeared on page one, stated, "Enormous meteorite drops down on Audubon Park." "A marvelous conglomeration of minerals and metals." "It woke up the people of Biloxi and Atlanta in its boisterous transit."

Having now obtained the attention of every reader, the article continued with eyewitness accounts of the incident. One Oliver McCool, night starter of the Prytania streetcar line, gave the following account:

> I went out of the starting house and saw a mass of flame descending in my direction, but still very far up in the sky. I tell you I was scared out of my wits. There was a red center in the mass of fire, and forks of flame leaped out from it. Scarcely a moment elapsed ere the frightful object plunged right down above me and exploded. A noise was followed instantly by the thing striking not far from me in several

sections, and I was thrown from my feet into the gutter, where I hid several minutes, thinking myself dead and the world at an end.

When I got up and took courage to look about me, I saw quite a section of the park or meadow out there covered with red objects and flames. There was one big mass which spit fire and steamed and was still hot and spinning when I went off from the watch at 6:00. I was too infernally scared to go near the object, and my hair has stood up straight ever since.

Further descriptions of the incident were given by Fire Captain Joseph Deegan, in charge of the fire house at Magazine and Calhoun. He stated that firemen, answering an alarm, hesitated to throw water on the blazing visitor, not knowing what would happen if they did so. Mr. E.T. Leche, commissioner of public works, under instructions of the mayor, took possession of the field covered by the meteorite and fragments. Several policemen were detailed to guard the place. The commissioner said, "I shall immediately cause two iron picket fences to be erected around the meteorite. No greater attraction for a public park has ever descended from on high."

It is strange that this phenomenal event, covered in such detail by the *Times-Picayune*, was not mentioned in either the *Times-Democrat* or the *Daily City Item*. In fact, subsequent issues of the *Daily Picayune* did not even mention it. You see, the day the story was carried was April first— that's right—April Fools' Day.

But where did this rock—a strange rarity in these parts—come from? The answer is simply that it was a piece of iron ore brought to New Orleans from Alabama for the 1884–85 World's Fair. After the fair, as is customary, there was a sale, with everything of any value being sold. Of course, no one apparently had a use for this piece of iron ore, so there it stayed. Today it is located on the Audubon golf course between holes six and seven.

Further controversy regarding the piece of stone occurred in 1947, when two Tulane University professors gave conflicting analyses of the rock. One thought the rock was truly a meteor as popularly believed; the other thought it a mere chunk of iron ore. No doubt, the face of one of the professors was as red as the fiery tail of a real meteorite dropping to earth from outer space.

THE U.S. CUSTOMHOUSE—BUILT
ON A FOUNDATION
OF COTTON BALES?

The answer is not only "no" but emphatically "NO."

The foundation to be used for the U.S. Customhouse (the second largest federal building when it was constructed—the nation's capitol was the largest) was determined by careful examination of the foundation that had supported the previous Customhouse building that stood for thirty-one years on the same site as the present Customhouse.

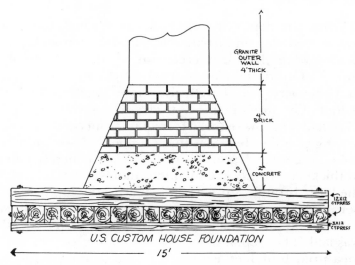

GRANITE
OUTER
WALL
4' THICK

4'
BRICK

2'
CONCRETE

12 X 12
CYPRESS

3 X 12
CYPRESS

U.S. CUSTOM HOUSE FOUNDATION

15'

A close inspection showed that the foundation was as good as the day it was put down. After this inspection was completed, an eight-inch diameter, twenty-seven-foot deep soil boring was made to test the soil. The first four feet were found to be a spongy vegetable substance; below that a stiff blue clay with a slight mixture of very fine sand was found. Based on these findings, on October 23, 1848, work officially began on the foundation that consisted of the following:

To keep the site dry during construction, sheet pilings were driven entirely around the square of ground. To make the joints watertight, cotton packing was used to seal the joints. A large number of cotton bales on the grounds where construction was taking place no doubt led to the popular but untrue belief that bales of cotton were used as the foundation of this massive structure.

The outside walls of the building are four feet thick. The inner walls measure two feet, six inches. It was determined that to support this structure the outer walls would have to have a footing that was eight feet deep and fifteen feet across.

When the depth of eight feet was reached, the ground was leveled with an instrument. Three-by-ten-inch cypress planks were then laid crosswise on the bottom of the trench. On these planks, twelve-by-twelve-inch cypress timbers were laid lengthwise close together and then bolted. On top of these, twelve-by-twelve-inch timbers were laid lengthwise three feet apart from center to center, leaving two feet between these timbers. These, too, were bolted together. Upon this grill was laid concrete two feet in thickness, firmly rammed into molds seven feet wide at the base, brought up perpendicular to the top of the timbers and then sloped one to one on the sides, reducing it to five feet on the surface. On top of the concrete, brickwork was laid. The step brickwork came up to ground level and measured four feet across, sufficient to receive the four-foot-thick outer walls. The same procedure, with the appropriate dimensions, was used for the inner walls. A total of 1,310,513 bricks were used for this purpose. In all, 18,500,000 bricks were used in the overall construction.

The engineer who designed the foundation fully realized that, due to the weight of the structure and conditions of the soil, there would definitely be some sinkage. He estimated twenty-four inches. To get an accurate reading, a gauge was installed. When the structure was formally completed in 1881, the building had settled thirty inches. Recent excavations have shown that the original ground surface was three feet, four inches below the present street curb.

In 1926, consideration was given to finishing the fourth floor of the building to provide additional office space. Before going ahead with the project, the foundation had to be checked to ascertain if it would be safe to add the additional weight. Diggings were made at two different points. The timbers were found to be as good as new, even though they had been in the ground since 1847. Extensive testing was completed, and the decision was made not to place any additional weight on the foundation. The project to finish the fourth floor of the building was abandoned.

In spite of the settling that has taken place, there are no serious cracks in any of the masonry walls in the building.

INTERESTING FACTS

Cornerstone and Cost

The city celebrated Washington's birthday on February 22, 1849, with a parade that ended at the Customhouse, with the highlight of the day being the laying of the cornerstone of the Customhouse by popular Henry Clay. The copper box placed into the cornerstone after being hermetically sealed held a message from the president of the United States, the constitutions of all states, a variety of coins, current newspapers, a directory of New Orleans, a medal of General Zachary Taylor, etc., etc. Historian Stanley Arthur tells us that the cornerstone was laid, undoubtedly, at the Canal and Decatur Street corner. Today, it cannot be seen because the building has sunk thirty inches and the street level has been raised three feet.

The cost of the building was $4,179,854. Construction began in 1848 and was officially completed in 1881.

In the early 1970s, serious consideration was given to demolishing the structure. In 1974, the building was placed on the National Register of Historic Buildings. In 1975, Congress appropriated $6,732,000 for restoration.

Architect

The federal government received numerous plans from architects who were most anxious to receive the contract. Renowned men like James Dakin, J.N.D. de Puilly, and Robert Mills were just a few. The winner was Alexander Thompson Wood, who was awarded the commission for his modified Egyptian building on September 22, 1847, despite the fact he had spent five years in a state prison for murder. The secretary of the treasury of the United States made the decision in favor of Wood for the following reasons: it was nearly the only plan which covered the whole ground; it was the least expensive and free from unnecessary ornaments; and it "combined all of the advantages of business."

Statues

Almost as heated as the arguments about the foundation of the building has been the discussion as to whether statues were ever meant to be placed in the twenty-four niches on the exterior of the building (six on each side). Most historians are in agreement that they were never part of the plan.

Lafcadio Hearn, a writer for the *Item* newspaper, wrote a most descriptive article entitled "La Douane" on December 2, 1878. He said in regards to the statues:

> Their rigid forms have never left the enclosure of the wooden coffins into which they were first placed for importation. They sleep in the awful silence and darkness of the most dismal chamber in the whole gray building.

Mr. Hearn was one of the city's most respected writers, and if he said there were statues, the masses believed him. Myth or fact—what do you think?

Exterior Columns

The magnificent columns on the outside of the structure (four on each side) are each carved from one entire block, and each weighs 105 tons.

The Marble Hall

The marble hall at the Customhouse when put into operation was termed "the finest business room in the world." It measures 95 by 125 feet and 54 feet high. The ceiling is supported by fourteen Corinthian columns 41 feet high and 4 feet in diameter. Each cost $15,000. The original shipment of marble capitals (each costing $8,000), which were to top off the marble hall columns, were lost when the sailing vessel *Oliphant* sank.

Lighting

Originally, the building was illuminated by gas. With Thomas Edison's invention of electricity, boilers were installed on the ground floor by the Edison Company in 1886, and electricity was provided to all parts of the building. It was not until 1939–40 that NOPSI (New Orleans Public Service, Inc.) furnished current to the building.

Roof

When the Civil War began, work was suspended and a temporary roof was installed and remained until work resumed in 1870. The great marble hall was not covered by the roof and a newspaper report stated, "Rain beats on the marble columns as freely as it does on the ruins of the Coliseum."

The original roof was made of copper. It took 85,000 pounds to cover the huge building. Copper proved to be unsatisfactory and caused endless problems, and was finally replaced with felt and asphalt pitch.

Main Entrance

The original plan called for the main entrance to be located on Decatur Street. Over the thirty-three years of construction, five different superintendents and four different architects served. Each man, of course, had his own ideas, and changes from the original plan were made before the building was completed. The current entrance on Canal Street is only one of those changes.

Mark Twain's Description

It simply reminded him of a large icebox.

"YOU SHOULDN'T EAT OYSTERS DURING MONTHS WITHOUT AN 'R'"

Almost every native Louisianian has heard the above from his or her parents or friends at one time or another. The reason, most surmise, lies in the fact we live in a semi-tropical climate, where ice and mechanical refrigeration was not available during the city's early history. It was believed your health would be in jeopardy if you had the audacity to eat oysters in a month without the letter "R." This is truly an old wives' tale, and has absolutely no validity.

In 1870, the Louisiana Legislature passed Act #18, which stated you could not sell oysters from April first through September fifteenth. This act came about because of numerous complaints that oyster reefs in coastal Louisiana were being rapidly depleted and destroyed (reason: demand was exceeding supply). In 1871, Act #91 reduced the oyster season, closing from May first to September fifteenth. Note that eighty-nine percent of the days in question are in months without the letter "R."

Therefore, the statement really should not have been "you shouldn't eat oysters during months without an 'R'"; it simply should have been stated that you *couldn't* eat them because you could not buy them due to the law.

To show how entrenched this belief was, the restaurant Antoine's, up until 1962, did not even offer the most popular dish on the menu, Oysters Rockefeller, during the months of June, July and August. This world-famous dish was invented in 1899 by Jules Alciatore at Antoine's Restaurant, and was so named because of the extreme richness of the sauce. Since the elder Rockefeller was then the richest man in the world, it was only natural that this rich dish should be named in his honor. To show the popularity of this dish, five million orders have been sold since its invention. With six oysters to the order, thirty million oysters have been consumed thus far in Rockefeller's name.

As outlined in Antoine's booklet by Roy E. Alciatore, Oysters Rockefeller is beyond question the "play" which has met with universal acclaim. More has possibly been written about this dish than any other food in the history of the world.

The state of Louisiana was one of the leaders in regulatory management of wetlands, dating back as early as 1857, when the general assembly (legislature) passed a law to protect game birds in St. Bernard Parish. It is because the oyster industry in Louisiana was regulated by the state that Louisiana today is the largest producer of oysters in the United States, averaging over ten million pounds of meat per year.

In Louisiana, fishermen cultivate oysters in 236,000-acre plots (called "water bottoms") leased from the state. Another one million acres of oyster grounds that are classified public beds are controlled by the state. The state has another 16,000 acres of state-controlled oyster grounds that are specifically reserved as oyster seed reservations.

Louisiana is not only the largest producer of oysters but also the largest consumer. This delicacy in Louisiana restaurants is available broiled, fried, smoked, smothered, and no doubt hundreds of other ways, some that many of us may never have heard of.

We don't really know who the first person on earth was to eat an oyster. We can only assume that individual had to be extremely hungry, for oysters in the raw are not the most appetizing sight. If we ever do find out who that person was, I highly recommend we dedicate a statue in his honor.

Oysters are a little like Howard Cosell. Almost everybody either loves them or loathes them. I personally don't loathe them, but love them on a loaf . . . or, better yet, in an oyster boat. This unique sandwich is fixed by baking a pan loaf of bread, and while it is still hot, pulling out the center of the loaf and saturating its innards with warm butter, then filling it with hot oysters and letting it sail off into your stomach—helped down at intervals with a gulp of cold Dixie beer. This experience could truly be called heaven on earth!

Today the best thing about oysters besides their taste is the fact that we can eat them every day of the year, including those months without the letter "R."

IS SPANISH MOSS A PARASITE?

Botanically, spanish moss is not a moss but a Bromeliad or a member, would you believe, of the pineapple family. Many visitors, as well as locals, find beauty and tranquility in the graceful streamers of spanish moss hanging from many trees in the Deep South. Spanish moss is found in abundance in the Deep South, for it thrives in a warm climate with high relative humidity. No doubt spanish moss is as close to heaven in our humid climate as it will ever get.

Actually, spanish moss is not a parasite, as believed by many, but an air plant. It does not derive anything from the trees upon which it grows nor is it harmful to the trees in any way. Moisture and dust from the air produce all the nourishment necessary to keep the plant alive and growing.

The plant absorbs water readily. It is, in fact, about 25 percent water. As frail as it might look, it is extremely hardy. No known insect will attack moss fiber, eat, destroy, or live within it. It appears that the only known enemy of spanish moss today is man, who has polluted the air in the name of progress.

Another unique quality of spanish moss is the fact that it is not propagated by seed but by fragments of festoons. The fragments are carried by the wind and birds from tree to tree. Birds frequently use strands of moss to build their nests, and, in this way, distribute the festoons.

How the Misconception of Spanish Moss Being a Parasite Got Started!

Not everyone, it seems, found beauty and tranquility in spanish moss. Some found it ugly and depressing. It became associated with the black plumes (symbol of death) used to decorate both funeral hearses and the heads of horses pulling the funeral hearses. Spanish moss, therefore, became associated with death, and this no doubt encouraged the belief that it lived off of and ultimately would kill the tree supporting it.

OTHER FACTS ABOUT SPANISH MOSS

How Much Produced

Huge cypress trees in the swamps of Louisiana have produced festoons of moss one hundred feet long. The

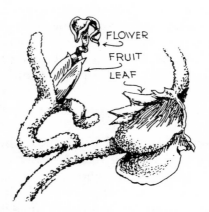

branches of a single giant oak tree at the mouth of the Atchafalaya River have been known to carry as much as twenty tons of spanish moss.

Fruit, Flowers, & Leaves

Although the human eye can barely see the tiny yellow-and-peach-colored trumpet-shaped flowers produced by spanish moss in the early spring, they are there in abundance. Spanish moss also bears fruit and produces leaves.

Where It Can & Cannot Live

Spanish moss will grow only in a tree; it will not grow on vines, wooden fences, telephone poles, buildings, or any other place except a tree.

It cannot live in a dead tree; once the tree dies, the moss dies and will soon turn black. It drapes itself in mourning as if for the tree, its dead mother.

Cushions

Because of synthetic materials produced today, there is only one moss gin still operating in Louisiana. It is located in Labadieville. This, of course, was not always the case. In

1927, Louisiana furnished 1,200 railroad cars of spanish moss to furniture, automobile, and airplane manufacturers for cushions. The spanish moss crop in 1927 was valued at two and a half million dollars, a sizeable industry at that time.

Mattresses

A mattress made of spanish moss is cool in summer, for air easily permeates the springy fibers. In our warm climate, this is a big plus. In winter, it is necessary to place paper under the moss mattress and an extra cover on top; otherwise it would be uncomfortably cool.

Medicinal

In 1884, a New Orleans guide book stated that "moss is the salvation of the swamp residents." In fact, "it feeds on the malarious elements in the atmosphere and consuming them purifies the surrounding air which, for human lungs and skin would be otherwise loaded with poison with a rapid decay of exuberant vegetation."

Bark

In the southern section of Louisiana, spanish moss has a light coat of bark and a heavy and long fiber. In the northern part of the state (over one hundred miles from the Gulf), the bark is heavy and the moss fiber is thinner. This is probably a protection against the colder climate.

Oddity

One curious feature of spanish moss is that it apparently has no beginning and no end. You might experiment and search in vain for hours; you will discover this to be a fact.

Where the Name "Spanish Moss" Comes From

Although the Louisiana Indians called the hair-like plant *itla-okla*, the French explorers thought it reminded them of the long, black beards of the Spanish explorers who had come before them, and renamed it. At first it was called spanish beard. This did not last long; the accepted name became and is still spanish moss.

THERE IS NO MYSTERY MONUMENT!

On a small, triangularly-shaped piece of ground surrounded by Esplanade Avenue, Bayou Road, and Tonti Street, there is a beautiful statue of the goddess of history perched on top of a unique terra cotta base. On the sidewalk, the title inset in the walkway in bold blue and white letters reads "Gayarre Place."

You would surmise that someone would read this and have an inkling of what the statue represents, or at least give them a lead to finding out. Unfortunately, grass covered the title for many years. People in the neighborhood began asking each other whom or what event the statue represented. In a sense, they became obsessed.

For a long time, it was an unknown to the area people, and a curious mystery. Someone suggested that they contact city hall. Many of them called city hall, and en masse received a standard city hall answer: "I don't know." The curiosity of the people, and their inability to find out what the statue was all about, led to the popular name that has lasted until this day—"the mystery monument."

Yet there really is no mystery. There is a simple explanation for the title that reads "Gayarre Place" that is inset into the walkway. Charles Gayarre (1805–1895) was the grandson of New Orleans' first mayor, Jean Etienne deBoré. As a child he spent most of his time on his grandfather's plantation, which is now Audubon Park.

Gayarre became a United States senator in 1835, but failing health forced his resignation. He traveled to France for treatment. In France, he did extensive research on Louisiana history, and wrote four volumes on the subject, which were later published in the United States. He was also successful in obtaining and returning to Louisiana many of the original French and Spanish documents relating to Louisiana's history.

Charles Gayarre was acknowledged as Louisiana's foremost authority and author on Louisiana history. In 1884, New Orleans hosted a World's Fair in what is now Audubon Park (formerly Gayarre property). Because of his renowned status as a Louisiana historian, a statue of the goddess of history was displayed on the grounds of the World's Fair in his honor.

After the fair closed, the statue was moved to its present location and the title was inset in the walkway beneath the statue, and to this day it reads "Gayarre Place." But we all know, no matter what the title inset reads, this monument will, no doubt, continue to be called the mystery monument.

You might say grass—not the kind smoked today—created a cloud of mystery that lingers around the statue till this day.

FIRST MARDI GRAS PARADE
IN THE U.S.—NEW ORLEANS,
LOUISIANA,
OR MOBILE, ALABAMA?

Each and every year prior to Mardi Gras, you will hear, at parties and wherever people gather, heated arguments as to whether the first Mardi Gras parades in North America, complete with floats, costumed riders, and flambeaux, were held in New Orleans, Louisiana, or Mobile, Alabama. Extensive research in libraries in both Mobile and New Orleans sheds the following light on the subject.

Early New Year's morning, 1830, in Mobile, Alabama, a group of young men were heading home after an evening which included plenty of libation. They passed a general store where merchandise was displayed out front. The group picked up shovels, rakes, hoes and cowbells, and walked down the street to the home of the mayor, where they raised holy hell.

The mayor invited them in, sobered them up, and offered the ring leader, Michael Krafft, a suggestion: "Next year, why not organize yourselves and let everyone have fun?" Michael formed a group called the Cowbellion de Rakin Society, after the instruments they used to raise hell. On *New Year's Eve* the next year, with costumed riders on floats lit by flambeaux, a *New Year's Eve* parade was held. Success was such that it was repeated as an annual event each *New Year's Eve*.

In 1856, members of the Cowbellions, now living and working in New Orleans as cotton brokers, decided to hold a Mardi Gras parade to entertain the crowds in New Orleans as they did in Mobile on New Year's Eve. They chose the name of the Greek god Comus, the god of revelry. They spelled it with a "C" to give it an English look. Since they would be a crew of men, they spelled it "Krewe" as a semblance of Greek influence.

On February 24, Mardi Gras 1857, starting at 9 P.M., the first Mardi Gras parade with floats, costumed riders, and flambeaux, all borrowed from Mobile, was held in New Orleans to the total enjoyment of the crowds. Ten years later, in 1867, the Cowbellion de Rakin Society moved their New Year's Eve parade to Mardi Gras.

THE OZONE BELT, SUPPOSEDLY NORTH OF LAKE PONTCHARTRAIN, IS A FIGMENT OF MAN'S FERTILE IMAGINATION

Very few topics of local interest have had more confusion regarding them, or less information about them, than the "pure, healthful" air of the "ozone belt" north of Lake Pontchartrain.

What makes it so confusing is the fact that Webster's original definition of ozone is as follows: "allotropic tri-atomic form O_3 . . . that is normally a faint blue irritating gas with a characteristic pungent odor." Ozone itself is considered dangerous, both to humans and agriculture, at levels greater than one tenth of a part per million. If exposed to ozone for excessive amounts of time, a human could develop lung disorders, hemorrhaging, and could even die. As you can see, this is powerfully potent stuff that you would certainly make every effort to avoid.

This being the case, why and how did the term "ozone" on the north shore of Lake Pontchartrain take on a positive instead of a negative meaning? The answer lies with two men, Captain Joseph S. Bossier and Colonel William Christy, both very capable, highly promotionally-minded, profit-oriented men.

The area north of the lake in the mid—1800s was a beautiful, heavily wooded area, with a reputation of being healthful because of the Abita Springs water that was believed to have medicinal powers. As the story goes, Abita, a beautiful Indian princess, fell in love with and married a handsome Spaniard of noble birth from New Orleans. She moved to New Orleans with her husband, fell ill, and no doctor or modern medicine could make her well. The

Choctaw Indians asked her husband to let them take her back to their village, saying that in one moon he was to come back and she would be well. He did as requested. At the appropriate time, he returned north of the lake, where he found Abita well and happy again (the word "Abita" in the Choctaw language means "fountain waters of health").

With this accepted legend of the phenomenal healing waters in mind, plus their knowledge of the terrible city conditions of New Orleans and other large cities in the South, especially during yellow fever epidemics, Bossier and Christy built a resort with comfortable summer cottages north of Lake Pontchartrain. With the healthy, cool spring waters available everywhere, plus a climate many degrees cooler in summer than hot and humid cities like New Orleans, the area was looked upon as a Garden of Eden. There were plenty of fresh eggs, milk, and butter, many streams, and Lake Pontchartrain, where fresh fish were bountiful. The people who came to the area to escape the miserable summers and the yellow fever epidemics were most pleased. Bossier and Christy prospered and were destined to become wealthy beyond their wildest dreams.

ABITA: "FOUNTAIN WATERS OF HEALTH"

"CRYSTAL CLEAR COOL
HEALING WATERS!"

"FRESH-SMELLING MEDICINAL
POWERS OF OZONE AIR!"

It is believed that the first association of ozone with healthful air came about when it was learned that when lightning strikes (and there is much of this north of the lake due to the large trees), the electrical charge compresses the oxygen and produces a form of ozone (this form does not have a negative influence on humans or animals). The two men, sensing the enthusiasm of the people for their resort, pounced on this opportunity like the Venus flytrap pounces on the unexpected victim who walks into its trap. Now they had another positive selling point to go along with the miraculous healing powers believed to come from Abita water. The one-two punch of publicity they used stated "crystal clear, cool, healing waters plus the refreshing, fresh-smelling medicinal powers of the ozone air make the area a virtual paradise."

The crowds accepted the term "ozone" without hesitation as being a healthy, positive thing. The resort was promoted nationally. People came from all parts of the U.S. in droves, resulting in the rustic cottages being replaced by luxury hotels. Steamboatloads of people lined the shores, where omnibuses waited to carry them to the nationally-renowned health spa. The area became so successful that by 1890 the Choctaw Indians were moved out of the area onto reservations in other states to make room for expansion.

As the old adage goes, nothing happens until something is sold. Without question, Captain Bossier and Colonel Christy did a yeoman's job of selling the outstanding qualities of ozone created by lightning, even though specialists in the environmental field tell us the amount of ozone created by lightning is infinitesimal and of as little help to our respiratory system as throwing a tooth-pick or straw to a drowning man.

Nevertheless, because of the phenomenal success of the area, and the association of the word "ozone" with fresh, clean air, *Webster's Dictionary* added a second definition that is in total contradiction to the first—that is, ozone (O3) as "pure and refreshing air."

THERE IS NO ST. EXPÉDITÉ

According to the records of the Catholic church, there is not now, nor has there ever been, a saint named Expédité.

But, you say, there is a statue in the old mortuary chapel that people pray to constantly, and they refer to it as St. Expédité.

This is all true, and there is a simple explanation as to why so many pray to someone who never existed. The confusion simply came from a lack of understanding of the Italian language by some French nuns. A large shipment of boxes containing religious articles was received from Italy for the chapel. One box was marked *E spedito*—meaning "send off" in Italian. Thinking this was a statue of a saint named Expédité—a French word—the statue and a small chapel were dedicated to St. Expédité.

Faith, it is said, is believing, not necessarily understanding. Thousands upon thousands have spent hundreds of thousands of hours praying to a saint that does not exist, and never has existed. With blind faith, no doubt the devotion to this non-existent saint will continue as it has for so many, many years.

CHAPTER 3

Metairie Cemetery

The Land
Metairie Cemetery Association
Architecture of the World
Various Professions Represented
Political Leaders
Unique Monuments
Final Resting Place for Politicians, Royalty, Military
    Leaders, and Madams

The Story memorial

A visiting writer to the Crescent City in the mid–1800s wrote, "Whenever I visit a city I have not previously visited, I always pay a visit to the city's cemetery before I meet the people. Experience has taught me you can learn a great deal about the people of that city by the way in which they treat those who have gone before them. After visiting a New Orleans cemetery, I knew without a doubt I was going to love the people of New Orleans."

Based on my personal experience in traveling to numerous countries throughout the world, his observation was right on the mark. I am also happy to say that as of this writing, Metairie Cemetery, in my humble estimation, is by far the most beautiful, most unique, and most historical of all the cemeteries I have visited in my lifetime. From a beautiful cemetery on a hillside in Athens, Greece, to the picturesque cemetery in the mouth of an inactive volcano in Hawaii, to the unique cemetery in Oberammergau, Germany, with its wooden markers that were hand carved by those buried beneath them, I have found there are many beautiful and unique cemeteries throughout the world, but Metairie still stands number one in my book.

Let me try my best to describe in words what makes this cemetery number one. I highly recommend that after reading this chapter you make a visit to the cemetery, for I am quite sure there are no descriptive words that can adequately capture the beauty, peace, and history of these sacred grounds.

THE LAND

The Mississippi River, over the course of thousands of years, changed directions six different times (see map page 72). Prior to its present location in New Orleans, the river flowed slightly to the north. When it changed its course, a small stream was left (see map page 72). Because of the natural levees built by recurrent flooding, this area was considerably higher than the surrounding area by

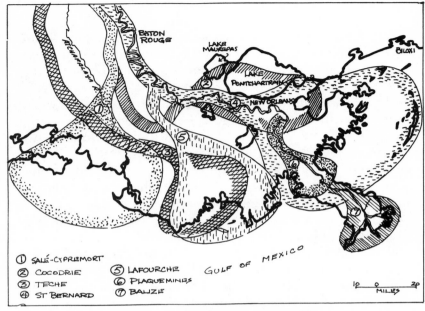

Different courses of the Mississippi River

① SALÉ-CYPREMORT ⑤ LAFOURCHE
② COCODRIE   ⑥ PLAQUEMINES
③ TECHE   ⑦ BALIZE
④ ST BERNARD

GULF OF MEXICO

The Mississippi River at the time of the founding of New Orleans

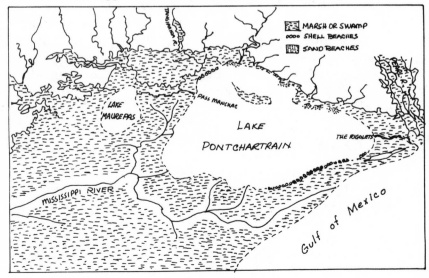

many feet, making it the only land in the city above sea level. When New Orleans was founded you could go from the Mississippi River to Lake Borgne and Lake Pontchartrain by way of Bayou Metairie, Bayou Gentilly, and Bayou St. John.

When New Orleans was founded, Acolapissa Indians lived on this high, dry land along the bayou. When food supplies ran short in New Orleans, the Indians sold food products to Governor Bienville. The French colonists called the area along the bayou where the Indians lived and raised their crops "la Metairie," meaning "the farms." Over the years, little by little, Bayous Metairie and Gentilly were filled in.

Both the Creoles and the Americans loved eating. Their passion for good-tasting, satisfying food was equaled by their love for horse racing. In 1838, the high, dry land on the ridge was purchased for a race track. It was called the Metairie Race Course, and consisted of a one-mile track and a grandstand 250 feet long. In a short time, it became the South's leading race track.

The New Orleans economy in that period in history was literally busting at the seams. Lloyd's of London and other notable houses predicted New Orleans would soon be the world's leading trading hub. Trade, as predicted, grew tenfold, and the popularity of the track did likewise. Attendance ranged from five to twenty thousand ecstatic racing fans. The place became so popular that special stands were built for ladies. They were plush and had parlors where the ladies could rest between races.

The highlight of the track came on April 1, 1854, when horses from Louisiana, Kentucky, Alabama, and Mississippi competed in a stake race. The race generated national and even international media coverage. Anyone who was anyone attended the gala, including U.S. President Millard Filmore. The principal horses were Ten Broeck's Lexington, the pride of Kentucky, and Lecomte, from the stables of Thomas J. Wells, a successful plantation owner from Alexandria, Louisiana (though for unknown reasons, Lecomte represented the state of Mississippi and not Louisiana). Both of these animals were remembered after their racing days ended. Lexington's skeleton is on display in the Smithsonian Institute, and one of Currier & Ives' most famous prints is that of Lexington. Lecomte was remembered in two ways as well. A town in Rapides Parish near Alexandria was named in his honor—although misspelled—plus a watch fob was made of the hair of his mane. It is in the possession of Mrs. Peggy Wells Hill, great-granddaughter of Thomas J. Wells.

When that unpleasantness called the Civil War raised its ugly head, the Metairie Race Course became known as Camp Walker, a Confederate Army training camp. When the war ended, every effort possible was made to restore the track to its former glory. The track was reorganized under the name "Metairie Jockey Club." Along with its new name, it also had a new board of directors.

No doubt economic conditions at the time were just too much to overcome. The story is told that in 1871, as a last ditch effort to save the track, an attempt was made to bring in Charles T. Howard, a wealthy, very influential citizen, who also happened to be the director of the powerful Louisiana Lottery Company. With his connections with the then hated Republicans, it was believed the track would not only survive but thrive. Members of the board were quite angry by this attempt, however, and Howard was blackballed. By 1872, there was nothing left to do but sell. On May 25, 1872, the sale was consummated, bringing an end to the famous racetrack. The new owners converted the land into a cemetery, run by the Metairie Cemetery Association. Sitting on the board of this new venture was none other than Charles T. Howard and his Louisiana Lottery business partner, John A. Morris. Someone surmised that Howard, with his millions of dollars and untold political power, was outraged at being blackballed, so in spite he turned the racetrack into a cemetery.

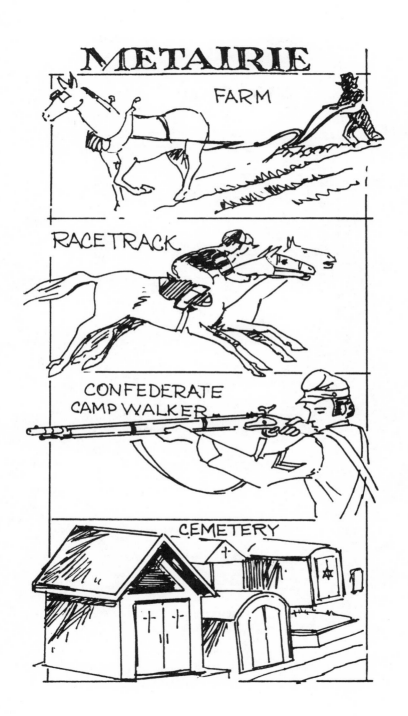

METAIRIE

FARM

RACETRACK

CONFEDERATE
CAMP WALKER

CEMETERY

METAIRIE CEMETERY

(Courtesy of Stewart Enterprise, Inc.)

METAIRIE CEMETERY ASSOCIATION

Colonel Benjamin Morgan Harrod, a prominent engineer with experience in cemetery promotion, was hired by the association. He quickly saw the opportunity to make a unique contribution to cemetery planning. On the irregularly shaped rectangle of ground, with roughly eighty acres to work with, he laid out a plan with expansion estimated to last at least one hundred years. It was no doubt an excellent plan, for many years after its 100th birthday the original plan is still being followed.

Harrod used the one-mile oval track (see drawing page 76) as the principal road around the cemetery. He then laid out other avenues of the cemetery to the same conformation. He designed three main ovals, bisected by cross avenues and triangles. Crossing the lagoons were picturesque stone bridges. Weeping willow trees were pianted on both sides of the waterways. These living symbols of sorrow made reflections in the still waters that were, it seemed, made for quiet moments of reflection and meditation. The place was truly beautiful, so much so that it became a popular place for entire families to go to take family photos.

ARCHITECTURE OF THE WORLD

As the years passed, the beauty of the cemetery grew. Massive monuments that served as enduring memorials to the deceased were built. Almost every conceivable style of architecture has been used within the confines of Metairie Cemetery. It has been said, "You need not go to the different foreign countries to see their architecture; simply go to Metairie Cemetery and your curiosity will be satisfied."

Islamic

Laure Beauregard Larendon was the daughter of General P. G. T. Beauregard. When she passed on, he had a

The tomb of Laure Beauregard Larendon

The Egan family monument

most unusually designed structure prepared as her final resting place. It is built of dark Belgium limestone. There are four Islamic horseshoe arches and a domed roof topped by an Eastern Orthodox cross bearing three arms.

Irish

During the Civil War, both sons of Mr. and Mrs. Henry I. Egan were killed at age 24. In their memory, the family had this most unique structure built. The design was inspired by ruins on the family's estate in Ireland. The structure was duplicated on a smaller scale in Metairie Cemetery. Every detail was copied to make it look authentic. Where there were cracks in the original, there are cracks in the one in Metairie Cemetery. It is unbelievable in its likeness to the burned and vandalized structure in Ireland.

Roman

Those who have had the good fortune of going to the Tivoli and seeing the Temple of Vesta will no doubt say "Bravo!" after seeing the replica in Metairie Cemetery. This striking memorial to Benjamin Saxon Story is a tribute to the artist who recreated it. One of the highlights of this monument is the urn in the center of the round pergola. The urn has two bands of magnolia blossoms carved in the granite.

On the side, you will see the inscription of Benjamin Saxon Story and his wife, Jeanie Campbell Story. Mrs. Story was a descendant of the Washington family, and, therefore, proudly displays her family coat-of-arms. The other two panels depict a sugar field and a scene that shows Confederate soldiers around a bivouac fire. Mr. Story operated a sugar plantation near Violet, Louisiana. He was also a proud member of the Confederate Army in its struggle during the Civil War.

The Tung family tomb

Oriental

There are a number of Chinese family tombs with oriental style architecture to be found in Metairie. One of them is the modified Chinese pagoda of the Charles Tung family.

The tomb of Mel Ott

VARIOUS PROFESSIONS REPRESENTED

Just as there are contrasting architectural styles within the cemetery, those who selected Metairie as their final resting place came from various professions and every conceivable walk of life. The following six diverse fields of endeavor are a good sampling.

Sports

The general consensus among those who are experts in the sport of baseball is that Mel Ott was the greatest baseball player ever to come from the metropolitan New Orleans area. He played twenty-two seasons with the New York Giants. During that span he had 511 home runs, 2,730 major league games, went to bat 9,456 times, scored 1,859 runs—including 488 doubles and 72 triples. He batted in 1,860 runs and retired with a lifetime average of

.304. When his playing days were over he became a successful manager of the New York Giants.

Gambler

Joseph V. Harrington was a master of his craft, which happened to be playing cards. While playing, his face was like that of a statue. He had the uncanny ability to study the cards in his hand without ever appearing to look at them. Because of these particular traits, he was given the colorful nickname, "Never Smile."

Harrington, one night in July 1924, had one of those nights when the cards seemed to run in his favor game after game. His winnings were astronomical. On his way home, he no doubt felt like he owned the world. Harrington's luck that night at the card table was as hot as it could possibly be. Unfortunately, his luck stayed at the table, for he was shot and killed by a holdup man that same evening.

In his memory, Mrs. Harrington had an imposing monument designed. The judge handling the succession refused to okay what he thought was an exorbitant amount of money, considering the value of his estate. Mrs. Harrington had the monument built just the same, and paid for it in cash in crumpled ten, twenty and hundred-dollar bills. Because of taxes his wife was no doubt given assets not known by any except "Never Smile" and herself.

Mariner

Steamboat captains loved their work as much as golfers enjoy their time on the links. Unlike golfers, who can never get enough leisure time, steamboat captains could never get their fill of their jobs. Captain LeVerrier Cooley, the last of the great steamboat captains, disproved the old adage "You can't take it with you." Upon his death, the bell of his last steamboat, the *Ouachita*, was permanently installed over his final resting place.

The grave of Captain Cooley

The grave of Edgar and Edith Stern

Edgar Stern's Loving Cup award, recreated in granite

Civic Leaders

Edgar and Edith Stern both had parents with highly successful business backgrounds. Mr. Stern enhanced the family financial position, allowing Edgar and Edith to spend both time and money serving the needy of the city. After Edgar's death, Mrs. Stern embarked on assisting the community and helping those in need, in proportions never matched in the city's history. With their endless help to the community during their lifetimes, each received the coveted *Times-Picayune* Loving Cups. The two cups, duplicated in granite, are on their tomb. They serve to remind us of the only husband and wife to achieve this feat. Edgar and Edith's final resting place, ironically, is very close to Longue Vue Gardens, their home while they were alive, and a gift to the city when they passed on.

Writer

December 16, 1951, was a sad day in New Orleans history, for this was the date of the death of one of New Orleans' best read authors, Elizabeth Meriwether Gilmer, better known to her millions of readers throughout the world as Dorothy Dix. For those too young to remember Dorothy Dix, she was the New Orleans lady who pioneered the newspaper column giving advice to the lovelorn.

Medical

Doctor Edmund Kells, the man who gave the greatest gift one can give to his fellow man—his life (see story on page 28).

POLITICAL LEADERS

Jefferson Davis

Only one American president has been laid to rest in Metairie Cemetery. Although not a president of the *United States* of America, he was, nevertheless, an American president. Davis was president of the *Confederate States* of America. Upon his death in New Orleans, Davis was placed lying in state for three days in the main chamber of city hall (now Gallier Hall). Endless lines came by to pay their last respects to their commander-in-chief.

His remains were appropriately placed in Metairie Cemetery in the tumulus of the Army of Northern Virginia, the same Army of Northern Virginia whose men fought and died to defend Richmond, the capital of the Confederacy. On the face of crypt forty-nine in the tumulus, in bold *gold* letters, was carved the signature of Jefferson Davis. At a later date, his remains were moved to Hollywood Cemetery in Richmond.

General Richard ("Dick") Taylor

Only one Louisiana resident ever became president of the United States. His name was Zachary Taylor. Although

Confederate monument in Metairie Cemetery that marks the spot of Jefferson Davis's burial

he is not buried in Metairie Cemetery, his son, General Richard ("Dick") Taylor, who fought so valiantly for the Confederacy, rests there.

Louisiana Governor Who Was Impeached

Henry Clay Warmoth, when only twenty-six, was elected governor of Louisiana. His term began in 1868 during the turbulent reconstruction era. It was during his administration that the state experienced its darkest political period. It was said Warmoth received a $6,000 per year salary; yet, after three years in office, he had a virtual fortune in his bank account. He was ultimately impeached.

The tomb of Governor Pinchback

The First Black Governor
to Serve in the United States

On December 9, 1872, upon the impeachment of governor Warmoth, President U. S. Grant appointed P. B. S. Pinchback governor of Louisiana. He became the first black governor of any state of the United States of America, and the only until Governor Douglas Wilder's election in Virginia. Pinchback died on December 21, 1921.

Louisiana's First Governor

In all, there are nine Louisiana governors buried in Metairie Cemetery. The first governor of Louisiana, William C. C. Claiborne, died on November 23, 1817, at the age of

42. He was originally buried in St. Louis No. 1 Cemetery. In 1880, his family built a tomb in Metairie and the Governor's remains were moved. It is interesting to note that when he died in 1817, there was very little fanfare, yet when his remains were moved to Metairie, they were done so in a great cortege. It is also interesting and somewhat bewildering that both of his wives (the first died when very young) are still buried in St. Louis No. 1 Cemetery.

Louisiana Governor Who Has a Town Named in His Honor

Michael Hahn, a German-born immigrant, was a brilliant young man. At age twenty, he received his law degree. His skills and drive led to his being installed governor in 1864, when Louisiana was partially occupied by federal troops. He was a strong-headed man who diametrically opposed the theme of his party and resigned his position. Hahn became an editor of a newspaper, and operated a plantation in St. Charles Parish. He was honored by having a town in Louisiana named for him. It is Hahnville.

UNIQUE MONUMENTS

When riding or walking through Metairie Cemetery, you will realize that there are numerous beautiful, eye-pleasing, and unique monuments. Some examples are as follows:

Captain Salvatore Pizzati

Captain Pizzati was an Italian immigrant who had a keen business sense and unbridled energy. He was the leading importer of tropical fruits for many years. With his exceptional ability and energy he amassed a fortune. Before he died, he requested in his will that he wished to be buried with his favorite rocking chair. As he wished, it was buried with him in the receptacle of the tomb below the crypt where he was placed.

The tomb of Captain Pizzati

The tomb of George and Eliza Nicholson

George and Eliza Nicholson

In life, they worked side by side. Today they rest side by side. On their monument, under each name, is inscribed "Manager" and "Editor of the *Picayune*." Eliza had the distinction of being the first woman in the United States to be the editor of a major newspaper. On top of the monument in bronze is a copy of an old *Daily Picayune* newspaper. Unlike most newspapers, this bronze one will last for many, many lifetimes. George and Eliza died just 11 days apart, on the 4th and 15th days of February 1896.

Mrs. Babette Vonderbank Ahrens

When Mrs. Ahrens passed away, a beautiful monument was built for her. The outstanding figures, besides the statue of Memory and a portrait plaque of Mrs. Ahrens, are the two life-size statues of her grieving niece and nephew. They are looking at her portrait. Below the portrait are the words "Dear Tante Babette."

J. R. Beckwith

Although the curtains on the bronze tablet are held open by two hands, and J. R. Beckwith's date of death is not inscribed, the curtains could be closed, for he passed away in 1912.

Augustus Bernau

If you would like to know what was said at the laying of the cornerstone of the original entrance to the cemetery, all you need do is visit Bernau's tomb. He was the speaker for the event and his speech is on the back panel of the tomb. The tomb is a small Byzantine chapel he erected for his wife. He was a native of Greece, and the tomb is built on Greek soil he had brought in. In the domed cupola hangs a bronze bell. Originally, a chain attached to the bell went directly into the tomb. The bell was rung on certain anniversaries.

Clark Monument

In 1914 the *Times-Democrat* and the *Daily Picayune* were having financial difficulties. A merger was deemed necessary to save both papers. Charles S. Clark, a paper merchant, was given stock valued at $7,000 instead of the money owed him. He apparently felt this was better than nothing. He tried selling it, but nobody wanted it. It turned out to be a godsend, for in 1963 the $7,000 of stock that he received in 1914 was valued in excess of $3,000,000. This magnificent monument has a large bronze plaque of the *Pieta* on a highly polished block of black granite.

The grave of J.R. Beckwith

James H. Hearn

Mr. Hearn was a very successful man in the coffee business, and a prominent and respected civic leader. Above all, he was no doubt a horse lover, for he selected the sight of his final resting place because it is the exact spot where he watched the races when he attended.

The grave of Mortimer Elkan

The headstone of Blaise Michael Carriere

Mortimer Elkan

This monument is self-explanatory, in view of what the party entombed did for a living. The bridge chiseled in stone stands out like a sore thumb. The six words at the bottom of the monument tell the whole story.

"He built bridges and built well."

Thomas L. Bayne

We all know the number one contact sport in New Orleans today is football. We all also know the number one non-contact sport is now and always has been politics. The father of Louisiana football was T. L. Bayne. In his college days, he was a star quarterback at Yale. Because of his love of the game, he brought it with him when he accepted a teaching assignment at Tulane University. He was virtually a one-man gang. He laid out the field, put up the goalposts, coached the team, sold tickets, and officiated at the games. He is also credited with choosing Tulane's colors and first school cheer.

Blaise Michael Carriere

A man who always had a smile on his face and a boutonniere in his lapel, Blaise was a relentless worker in both his job and causes he believed in. His love of children led him to be co-founder of NORD (New Orleans Recreation Department), one of the city's finest youth programs. The design of the monument was prompted by an award he received in recognition of his efforts in behalf of the American Legion-Junior Sports Association Baseball Program. Of course, the smile and boutonniere are there for all to see. The headstone was designed by his loving daughter.

FINAL RESTING PLACE
FOR POLITICIANS, ROYALTY,
MILITARY LEADERS, AND MADAMS

Metairie Cemetery is the final resting place for four chief justices of the Louisiana Supreme Court, eight mayors of the city of New Orleans, nine governors of Louisiana, fifty-one kings of Carnival, and who knows how many queens. Queens are mostly young debutantes who, upon marrying, take the names of their husbands, making it more difficult to trace them than tracing the kings of Carnival and Mardi Gras. The cemetery is filled with military men who defended us from our enemies, as well as many police officers who protected us from the criminal element, including the city's first chief-of-police, David Hennessey. The finest furniture-maker in New Orleans history, Prudent Mallard, rests here, we hope as restfully as the thousands who till this day comfortably rest in the famous beds and other furniture he built. Yes, from Josie Arlington, the famous red-light district madam, to Pendleton Lehde, who made a fortune in building radio stations around the world, and then gave of his time, talent, and money making New Orleans a better place to live, Metairie is blessed with counting amongst its numbers a great many of the movers and shakers that made our city a place so good, even the people who knock it constantly wouldn't think of living anywhere else.

CHAPTER 4

Code Duelo

CODE DUELO

The purpose of dueling, we are told, was improving morals and character. Unfortunately, there were thousands upon thousands of men who tried to defend their character and wound up as dead characters on the field of honor.

One-on-one combat is as old as mankind. When David slew Goliath, it went down as one of history's most memorable one-on-one duels.

Dueling became fashionable to defend one's honor because of two kings. Frances I challenged Charles V to a duel in the year 1528. Even though that particular duel never took place, other young officers took up the practice of fighting to uphold personal honor. In a short time, it became the vogue. In fact, it became so popular during the reign of Henry IV, 4,000 courtiers and officers of the army killed each other in duels. Laws were enacted against dueling, but were ineffective. Instead of dying out, the practice spread throughout the world.

By the 1800s, with the arrival of immigrants from Santa Domingo, and later officers and soldiers of Napoleon's army, New Orleans became the capital of the world for dueling. During the 1830s, more duels were fought in New Orleans than any other city in the world.

EARLY NEWSPAPER ACCOUNT
OF A DUEL

Chances are there were many who took part in duels and many who died prior to the first newspaper report of a duel in New Orleans. Among the earliest reports, on February 15, 1805, the *Louisiana Gazette* reported "the unhappy fate of Mr. M. G. Lewis, brother-in-law of Louisiana governor William C. C. Claiborne and brother of the late Mrs. Claiborne, who fell on Tuesday last in a duel with Mr. Robert Sterrey." The article went on to say that "Mr. Lewis

was a youth of amiable deportment and promising character." Sterrey was a writer for the *Gazette*. He wrote an article that criticized the governor for engaging in festivities so
soon after his wife's death. Lewis was enraged and challenged Robert Sterrey. The *Gazette* wrote:

> The parties met and were to wait the count of "one, two,
> three, fire." But Lewis' pistol flashed at the word "three,"
> and he lost his chance to fire. Mr. Sterrey, seeing this, im-
> mediately turned and fired backwards in the air. No offer
> of accommodation was made, and the parties again fired at
> the same moment. Mr. Lewis received the ball which
> passed through his heart, and uttering the words, "I be-
> lieve," he fell a lifeless corpse.

Mr. Lewis was buried the next day, and his funeral was
attended by a "large concourse of the most respectable
inhabitants."

POLITICS

William C. C. Claiborne, Louisiana's First Governor, Took Part in a Duel

Governor Claiborne told President Thomas Jefferson
that if he had known of his brother-in-law's challenge by
Robert Sterrey he would have prevented the duel. But
soon after Lewis's death, Claiborne found himself on the
field of honor. Once again the cause was an article in the
Louisiana Gazette.

In December 1806 Daniel Clark made a statement in the U. S. House of Representatives that "the militia of the Territory has been neglected and has seen a black corps preferred to them." This statement was quoted in the *Louisiana Gazette*. On May 23, 1807, five months after the article appeared in print, Claiborne demanded a retraction from U.S. Congressman Daniel Clark.

The very next day Clark wrote and refused to retract or explain his statement, even though he was not quoted exactly. With no retraction, Claiborne demanded satisfaction on the field of honor. For unknown reasons the duel was fought out of town. Nevertheless, the New Orleans *Gazette* of June 12, 1807, carried this squib:

> A duel was fought June 8, 1807 near Manchac Fort between Governor Claiborne and Daniel Clark, Esq. At first fire the governor received Mr. Clark's ball through his right thigh. His excellency has reached town and is out of danger.

It appears that a number of duels were fought because of articles written in the newspapers, and not only political articles. It was also extremely difficult for writers who covered the theatre and the opera. If they wrote unfavorably about an opera singer or a performer in the theatre, they were invited to the field of honor. If they refused, their only other choice was to leave town. Duels became so common that fathers dueled sons, brothers fought each other, and fathers-in-law and sons-in-law duels were quite common.

New Orleans Mayor
Kills U. S. Senator

The 1843 election waged by the Whigs and the Democrats was a violent political contest. In the course of the campaign, Louisiana's U.S. senator, George A. Waggaman, was killed in a duel by onetime New Orleans mayor Dennis Prieur.

Victims Become Political Supporters

To take part in the political arena in New Orleans without being involved in duels was next to impossible. U.S. Congressman Emile La Sere of New Orleans found a way to use the unavoidable duels to further his political career. Emile was miniature in size. He was about the height and weight of a fourteen-year-old boy of his day (1800s). Yet, in spite of his size, he survived eighteen duels, and at the same time won the hearts and votes of his constituents.

He made it a habit after each encounter to personally care for his opponents by bandaging their wounds that he himself had inflicted. He would also spend time at the bedside of his opponents as they recuperated. Many of those that he had bested on the field of honor became friends and ardent supporters.

FREEDOM OF THE PRESS

Newspaper Editor Shoots Newspaper Editor

On June 7, 1882, C. H. Parker, editor of the *Picayune*, had a duel with Major E. A. Burke, editor of the *Times-Democrat*. They fired pistols five times before Burke was

shot. Fortunately for Burke, he did not die from the gunshot wound. He lived and later became director general of the controversial 1884 New Orleans World's Fair.

There were those who felt it would have been better for the people of Louisiana had he been killed on June 7, 1882, for he left the country before the 1884 World's Fair closed with $1,777,000 of the fair's money, leaving the fair in a bankrupt condition.

Freedom of the Press
Taken Seriously

The great American statesman and orator, Patrick Henry, once said, "Give me liberty or give me death." One of the liberties he made reference to was freedom of the press. The editor of the *Picayune* newspaper, Jay Barnwell Phett, Jr., believed wholeheartedly in freedom of the press. He expressed this freedom in publishing an article that was contrary to the belief of New Orleans Judge William Cooley. Both men believed they were right and had the liberty to feel the way they did. So they decided to find out in a gentlemanly way who was right.

Patrick Henry's immortal words, "Give me liberty or give me death," were to be carried out to the letter. On July 1,

1873, Phett and Cooley met on the field of honor. The weapons selected were double-barreled shotguns. The editor of the *Picayune* took the liberty of proving he was right when he killed Judge William Cooley.

FENCING ACADEMIES

The golden era of dueling in New Orleans was from 1830 until the Civil War. The activity was so popular, and there were so many challenges made, it was only natural a man would take fencing lessons simply for self-preservation.

At this period in New Orleans history, Exchange Alley was by far the most popular spot in the entire city. The reason was that this is the area where all the great *maitres d'armes* (fencing masters) of the time had their schools. There were over fifty such schools in this small area. Upon passing Exchange Alley any afternoon, you could hear the rasping of the swords and the cries of the spectators who witnessed the contests. Every so often loud applause and cheers were heard.

The fencing masters in their day were as popular as, or possibly even more popular than, the rock or sports stars of today. They got the best seats at restaurants and received choice seats at the theatre. Crowds followed them, and when they went into a bar or coffeehouse, they were always guests whose money was never accepted.

One of the great instructors was Marcel Dauphin. His end was abrupt when someone he challenged, knowing he was outclassed, selected double-barreled shotguns at close range.

Bastile Croque're was considered the most handsome man in New Orleans, as well as an excellent teacher and duelist. He fought and won many duels in France but none in New Orleans. The reason was that he did not get challenged in New Orleans. He was a man of color, and no

white man would challenge him or accept his challenge. One of the rules of the Code of Honor stated: "You are required to challenge or accept a challenge of only those you would invite to your home as a guest or go to their home if invited."

Gilbert Rosiére of Bordeaux, France, was a lawyer by profession, as well as an excellent duelist. Shortly after arriving in New Orleans, he became an instant celebrity. In just one week, he was challenged seven times, went on the field of honor, and won all seven duels. He soon learned he could earn more money by opening a fencing academy than by opening a law office. He earned a fortune by teaching young army officers.

Rosiére was well-liked and respected. He was treated with all the courtesies of royalty. He was also as tender-hearted as he was efficient in his newly chosen profession. It was said he was so tender-hearted he would not kill a mosquito. He was a man who openly expressed his emotions. At the theatre and the opera, he frequently wept out loud—then calmly killed those men who openly laughed at what they called his feminine display of emotions.

FENCING MASTERS' TOURNAMENT

In the spring of 1840, it was decided a tournament would be held for only the fencing masters who had diplomas from recognized fencing schools. In this tournament, no doubt conceived at a bar filled with over-indulged patrons, half of the great fencing masters of the city were wounded or killed in short order.

Poulaga, an Italian who was believed to be the broad-sword expert, soon found out his title was not correct. Captain Themecoat, a French calvary officer, and Poulaga fought under the dueling oaks, using Poulaga's favorite weapon, the broadsword. It was one of the bloodiest duels ever recorded on the spot where thousands of duels took place. Captain Themecoat, with the precision of a surgeon and the quick moves of a gazelle, toyed with the Italian, slashing him at will. He literally hacked Poulaga to pieces, bit by bit.

NOT ALL WHO DUELED
WERE TRUE GENTLEMEN

One such rogue was Joseph Saul, cashier for the Bank of New Orleans. Saul was criticized for his banking activities by William Nott and Vincent Nolte, both directors of the bank. Saul had enough clout at the bank to have both men

ousted. Nott sent Nolte as his second to deliver the challenge. Saul, a proficient boxer, upon receiving the challenge, beat Nolte to a pulp with his fists, laying him up for several weeks. Nott immediately demanded Saul meet him the next morning for satisfaction, and Saul accepted. At ten paces, they both fired shots. Saul was wounded, but survived.

Nott, an expert shot, later found out why his straight and true shot had not killed his adversary. Saul, contrary to the gentlemen's rules as outlined in the Code of Honor, had his body wrapped tightly with ten yards of silk bandage. With many layers of silk to protect him, the bullet's velocity was slowed and the projectile was deflected, lodging slightly under one of Saul's ribs.

Saul proved, by beating Nott's second to a pulp with his bare fists, that he was not a true gentleman. Wrapping his body in silk doubly reinforced the conclusion that he was not a true gentleman. But, in the end, he was still alive. This was possibly the city's first flak jacket.

THE GREATEST OF THE GREAT

Señor Pepe Llulla, a proud Spaniard by birth, was considered to be the most accomplished duelist and teacher to ever walk onto the field of honor or instruct in a fencing studio. He was, without question, the finest swordsman who ever drew a blade in the Crescent City. He was equally capable with pistols, swords, sabers, and was a genius with a Bowie knife.

To demonstrate his accuracy with a pistol, he would place an egg on his young son's head and blow the egg to pieces every time.

With a rifle, he was awesome. He would demonstrate his skill with this weapon by having different people toss coins in the air at close intervals. He would hit twenty-five out of twenty-five on a regular basis.

In fact, he was so proficient in his trade, he was the only dueling master in the city that ever owned his own cemetery. It was said that his skill with every instrument of death allowed him to singlehandedly fill his own cemetery. The cemetery today is called St. Vincent DePaul, and is located on Louisa Street. This is also the final resting place of Pepe Llulla, his wife, and his daughter.

Yes, he lived a full life. He died on March 6, 1888, at age seventy-three. Yes, he died of natural causes. He was the last of the great fencing masters of New Orleans.

FOOTNOTE: Since Pepe had no paper signifying he graduated from a fencing school, he was not invited to compete in the fencing masters' tournament. He found out who objected to his participating, challenged him, and left him in a horizontal position under the dueling oaks, seriously wounded.

WHERE DUELS WERE FOUGHT

During the years the French and Spanish occupied New Orleans, almost all duels were held behind the Church of St. Louis, now the St. Louis Cathedral. There was a cleared area there that was called St. Anthony's Square. After the Louisiana Purchase, a number of places were used. They included a slightly cleared-out area on Metairie Road called Les Trois Capetines. Other areas used were Bayou St. John Road, the fairgrounds, and the Carrollton Race Course, to name just a few.

The most famous dueling grounds were located on the plantation of Louis Allard, now the home of City Park. There was a nave of giant live oaks, beneath which the duels took place. As time went by, the accepted designation became "the dueling oaks." Today there is only one of the original oaks still standing. Beneath this giant oak can be found the grave of the onetime plantation owner, Louis Allard.

Over the years, literally thousands of duels were held on this historic spot. On a single Sunday in 1837, ten duels were fought under the famous oaks, three of which ended fatally.

Although very uncommon, there was a duel under the oaks on horseback. Colonel Schaumberg of the United States Army challenged Alexander Cuvilier. Both men were stripped to the waist. Their weapons were broadswords. Although both men were bloodied before the duel ended, neither man was killed. The only casualty of the day was Colonel Schaumberg's horse, which was killed when struck by a blow from Cuvilier's sword.

Dueling on horseback was not very popular, although there were a number of duels held in this fashion in New Orleans. It has been reported that New Orleans was the only city in the country where duels on horseback took place and were reported in the newspapers.

DEFENDING WIFE'S HONOR

Of the countless reasons for dueling, it appears defending a wife's honor was way down on the list. One noteworthy exception reported in the newspaper involved Baron Joseph Xavier Celestin Dufau de Pontalba.

In 1811, at the tender age of 20, Baron Pontalba (Tin Tin to his friends) married his sixteen-year-old cousin, Micaela Almonaster. Although they were cousins and both were born in New Orleans, they were, nevertheless, strangers, for Tin Tin grew up in France. They saw each other for the first time just two weeks prior to the wedding.

Micaela's father was the late Don Almonaster. He was the wealthiest and most influential man in New Orleans. He built the St. Louis Cathedral and numerous other buildings after the disastrous fire of 1788. Tin Tin's family was equally prominent in France; as a boy Tin Tin served as a pageboy to the emperor.

The wedding was, at that time, the most brilliant ever held in the great cathedral. The guests were the cream of creole aristocracy. Micaela, in her beautiful wedding dress, looked like a doll. Her red hair beneath the pure white veil looked like flickering flames as she walked with equally fiery Bernard Marigny arm in arm down the aisle that was lit by thousands and thousands of candles.

After the wedding, the young couple lived in France at Mont L'Eveque with its grand *et-petit chateau* (now the American embassy). This was just one of the gifts of Micaela's father-in-law. The young couple were very much in love.

One evening while attending the opera in Paris, Tin Tin heard a man behind his wife make a derogatory remark about her. He instantly turned and verbally confronted the man. The next day Tin Tin sent his second to make necessary arrangements for satisfaction on the field of honor.

Pistols were selected as the dueling instruments. The time was set for dawn.

It appeared that dignity wore the face of a clown on that particular day. Tin Tin got off the first round, missing his opponent. Like the true gentleman he was, he dropped his arms to his sides. With ice water in his veins, he looked his opponent straight in the eye and waited for him to take careful aim and fire. Within seconds, the thunderous noise was followed by the pistol's projectile. It struck Tin Tin, but luckily for him, only a finger was lost. Blood was drawn. As they would say when this happened, "M'sieur's honor was satisfied."

Unfortunately, Micaela in a sense also took part in a duel. This one was not held with the strict rules of the Code of Honor. This was the result of a violent argument behind closed doors, and involved only one gun.

Micaela was a very strong-headed individual. The marriage had gone sour, and she wanted an annulment. Tin Tin's father was infuriated. He insisted she change her mind, as this would certainly ruin his family name. The more he demanded the more she laughed in his face. He could no longer tolerate her behavior. He lost control of his temper, reached into his coat pocket, took out a pistol, and carefully aimed at her at close range.

Micaela reacted quickly by placing one hand over her face and the other over her chest. The bullet took off one of her fingers that was placed over her chest, but did little other damage. She was young and he was an old man. With adrenalin flowing, she wrestled the gun from him and shot him through the head. He was dead before he hit the ground.

Micaela was never charged for the death of her father-in-law, and in the end did receive her annulment.

In looking back at the two incidents, both involving guns, Micaela and her husband each lost a finger, the husband lost a wife, and the father-in-law lost his life. It seems there were no winners in the end. After all the smoke had cleared, Micaela moved back to her beloved city of New Orleans and lived to the ripe old age of seventy-nine.

AMERICANS ADD NEW TWISTS

Before the Americans became involved in dueling in the Crescent City, the Creole's principal weapons were the colchenarde (a type of sword), the rapier, and the broadsword. They occasionally used the not-too-accurate pistol of the period. The Americans, upon entering New Orleans, were compelled by circumstances to take part in what was totally foreign to them: the Code of Honor. They quickly summed up the situation. The primary purpose of fighting a duel, they surmised, was to kill your opponent. They, therefore, used the deadly squirrel rifles, and even double-barreled shotguns loaded with slugs. They reasoned that if they were not a good shot, this would at least allow them a fair chance of killing their opponent.

Some uncouth Americans went as far as selecting clubs and axes when challenged. In 1810, one American, no doubt with a warped sense of humor, selected eight-foot-long, three-inch by three-inch square cypress timbers. That freakish battle found both men bruised, bloodied, and knocked half senseless. You could go so far as to say that with these instruments of destruction there was a good chance to be "board" to death.

A TRY AT OUTLAWING DUELING

When Bienville became governor of Louisiana, he did his very best to discourage dueling. His efforts were useless. When Governor Miro, a very successful Spanish governor, took control, he declared he would vigorously enforce all regulations against dueling. He had about as much success as Bienville. When Louisiana became part of the United States, an article was entered into the state constitution disenfranchising duelists. All of these attempts were about as successful as Prohibition was at keeping people from drinking alcoholic beverages. There are some things that man just cannot legislate, no matter how hard and how long he tries.

Today without the rules of the Code of Honor to follow, there are possibly more people killed by guns and knives than ever before.

HUMOR

Even in events as serious as dueling, there is ample humor to be found. A few examples are as follows:

Take Care of Your Health

A true gentleman walked onto the field of honor during a rain storm. He had a pistol in one hand and an open umbrella in the other, declaring, "I am quite ready to be killed, but I do not wish to catch cold."

Harpoons at Twenty Paces

Harvey, Louisiana, located on the west bank of the Mississippi River just above New Orleans, is named for S. M. Harvey. He came to New Orleans in 1840 and married Miss Louise Destrehan of the wealthy and prominent family of that name.

Prior to coming to New Orleans, Harvey was a skipper of a whaling vessel. In his new environment of wealth and influence, and not knowing the intricacy of the Creole customs, he was as out of place as a New Orleanian carrying snow skis in August.

One evening, Harvey and his wife attended a gala dinner party that was followed by the customary gentleman's card game. The game proceeded quite pleasantly until an altercation arose between Mr. Harvey and a Creole gentleman of high position named Mr. Albert Farve. Mr. Farve did something that provoked Harvey, who, in an ungentlemanly fashion, punched Farve, knocking him to the ground and inflicting a black eye.

The next day, Farve sent his second (person selected to represent him according to the dueling code) to advise Harvey that he, Farve, had been insulted and wished to meet him in mortal combat on the field of honor. The second then advised Harvey that his being challenged allowed him choice of weapons. Harvey, being unaccustomed to the code duelo rules, asked for a further explanation. Farve's second responded, "You, sir, may select pistols, swords, rifles, shotguns, or any dangerous weapon in which you may be skilled." Harvey, thinking for a minute or two, then said, "I understand now and will meet your friend on the terms you state. Please pick the time and place to suit your own convenience."

Farve's second replied, "That, sir, is prompt and like a gentleman of honor." He then asked, "Please favor me with your choice of weapons that I might communicate it to my friend." Harvey very politely said, "Please wait a minute." He then went into another area of the house and returned with two ten-foot-long hickory-handled whaling harpoons. He advised the second that this was his choice and would be used at a distance of twenty paces. He then went outside and demonstrated the weapon by splitting a small tree in half at twenty paces.

The astonished and confused Creole gentleman questioned, "What, sir, do you suppose my friend to be—a fish to be stuck by such a damn tool as that?" "Fish or no fish," replied Harvey, "this is my choice of weapons." The indignant Creole left in great disgust and reported to his principal. After careful deliberation, Mr. Albert Farve decided he had not really been insulted by Harvey, and the proposed duel with the harpoons never took place.

In this instance, because of quick thinking and a sense of humor by Harvey, in place of blood being spilled on the field of honor, laughter spilled throughout the city as word spread of his unusual choice of weapons.

Oh, No, Not My Hat!

A French officer whose hat was punctured by his opponent's sword at the end of a duel was infuriated. He stated he would rather have had the sword through his body than through his hat. His reasoning was that he had a close friend who was a surgeon who he was sure would give him credit, but he knew no hatter that would.

We Will Duel Where?

Colorful Bernard Mandeville Marigny was a kind and lovable Creole gentleman. Two flaws in his character were his quick temper and intense jealousy.

One evening at a party at his palatial home in New Orleans, one of his longtime friends was joking with him as he had done many times in the past. On this particular evening, Bernard was in a foul mood, and his uncontrollable temper erupted. The next day, he sent his second to demand satisfaction on the field of honor.

The old friend that he challenged was a giant of a man who stood six feet, six inches tall, a full foot taller than his challenger. He was, in a sense, a true paradox, being as strong as an ox and at the same time as gentle as a kitten.

After considering the challenge, and knowing Bernard's quick temper, he chose as weapons ten-pound sledgehammers, with the duel being fought in six feet of water in Lake Pontchartrain.

Marigny's second returned and reported the choice of weapons and the location of the duel. Marigny, with a stern look on his face, at first became very silent, then smiled slightly, finally laughing uncontrollably at what his wise and witty friend had proposed. The two men did meet and instead of inflicting bodily harm on each other, they simply hugged each other.

She Won't Dance, Don't Ask Her

As a young man, on one of numerous business trips to Mobile, Bernard attended a gala party, where he instantly fell in love with a beautiful young Creole maiden whom he later married. On the very evening he met her, he insisted she dance with him and no one else despite the names on her dance card. Because of this dictatorial and unacceptable behavior, during the course of the evening he received no less than six challenges, which he gladly accepted.

Bernard was a very small man; all six of his opponents were superior to him in size and strength. With the speed of an expert pickpocket, the grace of a ballerina, and the skill of a surgeon, in short order he literally tore his first opponent to shreds. He could have actually killed the man had he wished to do so, but he did not.

After seeing what had happened to what was believed to be the best swordsman of the six challengers, the other five reconsidered their positions and found they were not really offended as much as they first thought. Like Bernard said—"She won't dance, don't ask her."

Thanks, I Needed That

Alexandre Grailhe of New Orleans was seriously wounded in a fencing duel with Mr. Donatien Augustin. His lung had been punctured and an abscess had formed. Grailhe was bedridden and near death for months. Miraculously he survived, but his affected organ left him bent over like an old man. He soon had the misfortune, which later became good fortune, of being challenged to another duel, this time by Bernard Mandeville Marigny.

Because he was weak and could not stand erect, Grailhe chose pistols as the dueling weapons. Marigny's shot was right on the mark, puncturing Grailhe's lung and opening the abscess. This quirk of fate brought about his total cure, and from then on he walked erect and proud.

The second duel not only straightened him up physically, it straightened him up otherwise. After his second duel, his name never appeared again in the newspaper listing of duels in the Crescent City.

LAST RECORDED CHALLENGE

The last recorded challenge to a duel in New Orleans was as recent as April, 1908. Mr. J. B. Honor felt he was dishonored by a quote made by Mathew J. Sanders. No doubt Mr. Honor felt that just because Sanders was Rex (king) of the 1902 Mardi Gras, whose parade theme was "Quotations from Literature," this did not give Sanders the right to make a quote that belittled him. J. B. Honor sent his second, who offered a choice: a public apology or a duel on the field of honor. Sanders had no intentions of apologizing. He also declined the challenge, saying dueling was out-of-date, plus he was a man of peace. Honor was infuriated and took out an advertisement in the newspaper calling Sanders a poltroon. No doubt his royal highness believed the old adage, "Sticks and stones may break my bones, but words will never hurt me."

Keeping a cool head in dealing with a hothead, Mathew J. Sanders proved he was not only the king of Mardi Gras in 1902, but a prince of peace in 1908.

CHAPTER 5

Statuary

Autumn

Summer

Winter

Spring

This chapter on New Orleans statues is far from covering all of the statues in the city. To do that would require a book in itself. Our aim is to cover a cross section, and thereby give a sampling of what is on display for your enjoyment. As you drive around town, you will notice some of those we cover and many that are omitted. Our hope is that as you pass those covered it will spark a rememberance of that person and what they accomplished, and possibly encourage you to emulate their good deeds. For those you do not know, we hope it will spark your interest to find out their particular story, for all of our statues have interesting stories, and most are inspirational.

When studying the statues of New Orleans, one thing stands out like a sore thumb: almost all of the statues dedicated to someone are there because of what the person gave during his or her lifetime, not what he or she received. This confirms the old adage, "It is better to give than to receive." Those who give of their time and their talents to their fellow man are remembered long after those who are simply on the receiving end.

STATUARY NEW ORLEANS

Although present-day New Orleans is blessed with numerous outdoor statues that serve as reminders of our glorious past, it is ironic that there was not one statue placed in the city by either France or Spain, who, combined, ruled the city of New Orleans for eighty-five years. This is rather odd when you consider most European cities are up to their armpits in statues.

Although there are more statues dedicated to military personnel than any other category, with virtually every military conflict covered, whether it was a war or a "police action," strangely there is not one statue within the city of New Orleans dedicated to a hero who fought in World War II.

Equally curious is the fact that even though Mardi Gras parades and jazz music were both born in New Orleans, and our port has been the main economic artery from the city's earliest history, there are no statues dedicated to those who made our city the Carnival and Mardi Gras capital of the world, and no statues of those who worked in the maritime industry. Worse still, would you believe there is a statue for only one out of all the hundreds of great jazz musicians who have honored our city by bringing jazz to every corner of the world? Aside from these deficiencies in honoring the great men, women, and events of our city, our area is more than adequately blessed with statues in other categories.

FIRST PROPOSED OUTDOOR STATUES

When designing the U.S. Customhouse for New Orleans in the 1840s, the original proposal submitted included twenty-four statues that were to be placed in concave areas designed into the outer walls at sidewalk level. Over the thirty-three-year period that it took the building to be completed, many of what were called unnecessary frills were removed from the original plan in order to reduce the cost. Unfortunately, the twenty-four statues were never put on the final plans, and their empty niches remain only a fond memory of what could have been but never came to be.

FIRST STATUES

The city's first statues were an example of one of those strange quirks of fate. The quirk lies in the fact that New Orleans' geographic location means it falls into the semi-tropical category. We do not enjoy the four seasons as other parts of the country do. It is quite common for us to go from summer to winter in just one day. With a few exceptions, fall and spring just seem to pass us by in the wink of the eye. Living in a semi-tropical area, we are blessed with a short winter season. Last year it was on a Wednesday, in the afternoon, late.

As fate would have it, the first outdoor statues displayed in New Orleans other than cemetery statues are located in the four corners of Jackson Square. These four statues, would you believe, represent the four seasons of the year. Ironically, the statues represent the one thing New Orleans has never enjoyed. The placing of the city's first statues was apparently not considered a big deal by the city fathers or the local newspaper. The *Daily Picayune* on June 20, 1852, devoted just one paragraph to the event. It read:

> Marble statues received several months previously from the north were set up in the corners of Jackson Square on white marble pedestals, representing winter—an old bearded man, muffled in a cloak; spring—a young girl, holding flowers; autumn—a native mature woman, sickle in girdle; summer—a young man, legs crossed, book at breast, luxuriant grapes resting on what appears to be a tree trunk on which he leaned.

The statues were, no doubt, part of the renovation of the square, which included changing the name from Place d'Armes to Jackson Square in 1851. The present iron grill fence was erected that year and the base of the proposed statue of Andrew Jackson was moved from a spot a little to the left of the center to the exact center.

MOST PHOTOGRAPHED STATUE

Without a close second, the statue of Andrew Jackson in Jackson Square is the most photographed and admired in the city.

The picturesque fourteen-foot, fifteen-ton bronze statue (one third larger than life) is the work of Clark Mills. Mills was born in 1815 in New York state, and was left an orphan at the age of five. He had no formal education, yet, no matter whether the job was laborer, carpenter, teamster, etc., he was able to master all that he undertook. He was, in the truest sense, a jack-of-all-trades.

Clark Mills

While still a young man full of confidence, he learned the skills of an ornamental plasterer. This was the first step in his career as a renowned sculptor. In 1848, just by chance, he met U.S. postmaster general Cave Johnson. Knowing of Mills' work as a sculptor, Johnson suggested that Mills submit a design for an Andrew Jackson memorial that was approved for Washington, D.C. Mills had never before done a full human figure, and he knew absolutely nothing about casting in bronze. He thought to himself, "What can I lose by entering the competition? After all, I am a jack-of-all-trades, and if I receive the commission, in time I know I can master this project as well."

Through research, he learned that Jackson was a man of action; therefore, the statue he proposed was General Jackson on a rearing horse. His bold concept won him the $20,000 contract to create and cast in bronze the first equestrian statue in the U.S. He now had to achieve that which defeated sixteenth-century genius Leonardo da Vinci. He had to support the great weight of horse and rider on the slender hind legs of the animal.

Mills experimented for three years. He purchased a Virginia thoroughbred, which he trained to stand on its hind legs and remain in that position so he could capture the correct stance of the animal. In time, Mills found the solution to supporting the great weight. He explained in 1856 while in New Orleans:

> The mode in which the statue sustained itself on its hind legs is on the simple principle of equipoise—that is, drawing a vertical line from the front of the hind hooves upward, the amount of metal on one side of it is equal to that on the other.

In other words, he designed the horse and rider so that the maximum weight stood over the hind hooves, with the rump of the horse outweighing the forepart.

When he finished casting the statue, it was made up of some sixty parts. The largest parts are the horse's head, forequarter, and hindquarter. The figure of Jackson is made of many parts; the head, upper body, forearms, hat, legs, and boots are all separate parts. The parts are cleverly assembled with drift pins in such a way as to make the statue appear to be one solid piece. The statue in Washington was dedicated on January 8, 1853, the thirty-eighth anniversary of the Battle of New Orleans.

New Orleans Statue

On Jackson's last visit to New Orleans in 1840, he laid the cornerstone (left of center in the square) for a monument in Place d' Armes.

In 1852, the New Orleans Jackson Monument Association was organized. The first order of business was, naturally, the collection of money. Even though the state treasury donated $10,000, the association was far short of the estimated $28,000 needed (excluding base). Learning of the Mills statue of Andrew Jackson, the members felt that if they could get him to duplicate the statue, for which he already had a mold, they could get a good price. Mills was contacted and asked if he would be interested in furnishing the monument and base in New Orleans. His answer was in the affirmative.

In 1853, the association received another $20,000 from the state. On June 15, 1853, it was unanimously resolved to entrust the execution of the statue and base to the renowned and highly respected Clark Mills. Mills accepted the commission and agreed to complete the project in three years.

In 1854, Mills came to New Orleans and subcontracted the statue's base to Mr. Newton Richards. In October of 1855, as Mills was nearing completion of the statue, work on the base began. On October 30, members of the association relocated the cornerstone that had been laid by Jackson in January of 1840, and placed it inside the brickwork of the new monument base. The cornerstone was a granite block, hollow in the center, which contained a copper box filled with items put there by Andrew Jackson. Hundreds of citizens who heard of what was taking place went to the square and asked that the copper box be opened. The commission members refused.

Besides the copper box from 1840, a second one was placed in the brickwork. It contained the transcript of the association's first meeting on January 11, 1851, a copy of Louisiana's Civil Code, a brief history of Andrew Jackson, coins, and many other items.

When it was learned the statue and base would both be finished ahead of schedule, the date of January 8, 1856, was set for the dedication. As the old saying goes, "The best laid plans of mice and men can sometimes go astray." The ship carrying the statue ran into problems, and the January date could not be met. A new date of February 9 was set. Naturally this great occasion called for a massive parade, which included many of the men who fought at the famous Battle of New Orleans in 1815. Numerous military bands, politicians, religious leaders, plus every organization, be it civic, social, or business, took part. Of course, Clark Mills, the creator of the statue, was in that number.

After the parade, the square was filled to capacity. Those who gallantly fought at the Battle of New Orleans received the most honored positions. The streets and buildings surrounding the square were equally jammed with people. A platform was installed in front of the covered statue. From this lofty spot which all could see, L. J. Sigur delivered an appropriate address. He was interrupted by frequent applause of those who could hear him.

Upon completion of his talk, a rope was pulled, releasing the covering on the statue. As it fell to the ground, the bright sun illuminated and highlighted the bronze figure of Jackson and his trusty steed. Immediately, thunderous cheers of joy filled the air. Hats of the men and handkerchiefs of the ladies waved vigorously. The many bands joined in the celebration with music that further excited the crowd. Cannons on the levee fired a one hundred-gun salute as church bells rang.

All finally quieted down. Like a conquering hero, Clark Mills was next to mount the podium. He described his work and explained details of the statue. His address was printed word for word in the newspaper the following day. Upon completion of his speech, the crowd once again

Statue of Andrew Jackson

broke out with cheers of appreciation. Later that evening, the celebration came to an end with an elegant dinner held at the palatial St. Charles Hotel.

The final cost of the statue and base in New Orleans was $30,000. That was $10,000 more than the identical statue in Washington, D.C. Needless to say, the Jackson Monument Association in New Orleans did not get the bargain they expected.

There is a third statue, located in Nashville, Tennessee, which is identical to the first two. This one cost only $5,000. It is believed that this was the first statue cast, and was rejected by Mills. Doubtless he later decided that it was worth at least this amount.

The only difference in the three statues is that the statue in Washington was cast in part with bronze from enemy cannons captured by Andrew Jackson. Or was the rejected statue, the first one cast but rejected, and later sold to Nashville, the one with the special bronze?

Defaced Base

When New Orleans fell during the Civil War, Major General Butler, commander of the occupation forces, quickly became an unpopular man. After all, he hung Mr. Mumford, an irate citizen, for removing the American flag from the U.S. Mint building, put the mayor of the city in jail, and banished some religious leaders. For these and many other dastardly deeds, he was called "Butler the Beast," along with many other unkind names. He took his resentment out on the people by having the following words chiseled into the base of the ever-popular statue of Andrew Jackson: "The Union must and shall be preserved."

No doubt, during Butler's stay in Washington, he saw an inscription on the base of the Jackson monument which was a quotation of Andrew Jackson while president of the United States. Jackson gave a toast on the birthday of Thomas Jefferson which went thusly: "Our federal union—it must be preserved."

Although Butler's addition to the statue was not word for word, he knew that the sentiments would certainly ruffle the feathers of all the Southerners who were now under his thumb.

Name on Statue

For many years, there was no inscription on the base of the Jackson monument. Finally a three-by-eight-foot bronze plate with the inscription "General Andrew Jackson" was added. It fell off and lay in the flower bed until 1935.

Finally, on August 26, 1982, "Major General Andrew Jackson" was sandblasted into the base of the statue.

The Day Andrew Jackson
Lost His Head

Early in the morning on Friday, February 23, 1934, people walking through Jackson Square were shocked when

they looked up and saw a headless Andrew Jackson. Everything else was there. He still saluted with his hat, but his head was gone.

It was learned that on the previous night some mischievous boys were playing around the statue. One of them with a little monkey in him scaled the monument, loosened the drift pins holding the head to the body, and knocked it to the ground.

Luckily, a state museum porter found the head on the ground that same evening and took it to the Cabildo for safekeeping. Close examination showed only a minor scratch on the eyebrows. A plaster cast was made of the head as insurance in the event that the General were ever to lose his head again.

In 1960, the General lost his saber to vandals. Unlike the lost head, it was never found. The saber of the identical statue in Nashville, Tennessee, was used as a model. A new one was made and returned to the General's side.

The only missing part of the statue today is the spur on the General's right boot. Apparently, it has been decided that since the General isn't going anywhere, and the missing part is not that conspicuous, it need not be replaced.

MOVING STATUES!

When thinking of statues, one normally thinks of something that occupies a permanent location. This has not been the case in New Orleans statuary history. It is as though many of our statues were given life and moved themselves to another location. In some cases, several moves have been made. We are not saying moved and put back in the original location, as was the case of the Robert E. Lee statue.

In 1953, a new foundation was needed for the Lee statue. The 7,000-pound, sixteen-and-a-half-foot figure of Lee was taken down and placed in a wooden box, which was filled with sand for protection, and then stored in a warehouse. Once the new foundation was completed, Lee was once again placed on top of the ninety-foot granite shaft. Fifty-three was a bad year for Lee, for it was the only year that he missed seeing the Mardi Gras parades.

NOTE: As you go around the Lee monument on St. Charles Avenue, you pass the YMCA building. Tour bus operators are quick to point out, after telling the story of Robert E. Lee, that the YMCA is there as a reminder to the people of New Orleans that the Yankees Might Come Again.

Statues that have been moved from one location to another are:

Hercules

Once proud, always nude, Hercules originally occupied the center area of the entrance to the Delgado Museum of Art in City Park (now the New Orleans Museum of Art). His present location is to the right of the main entrance of the museum.

Hercules

Monument to John McDonogh

John McDonogh

This great nineteenth-century businessman is the only New Orleanian who has two statues dedicated in his honor. Although eccentric and considered miserly during his lifetime, he did leave the bulk of his huge estate to public schools in New Orleans and Baltimore. All he asked in return was that school children be allowed to place flowers on his monument on May 1 of each year. His request has been carried out each and every year, with the only exception being 1989, when heavy rain caused cancellation.

Originally, the ceremony took place at the McDonogh monument in Lafayette Square. When the new City Hall was built across from Duncan Plaza, the ceremony was moved to the plaza. During the Great Depression, a bust of McDonogh was commissioned by the W.P.A., and was placed in a small uptown park located on St. Charles Avenue and Toledano Street. In April of 1957, it was moved to Duncan Plaza and has been used for the McDonogh ceremony each year since. The bust initially faced City Hall. When Duncan Plaza was refurbished in 1989, it was necessary to move the bust to another location on the grounds. It is now located facing the State Court Building.

That's two moves for the bust of McDonogh, one more than his mortal remains. Upon his death in 1850, he was buried in the McDonoghville Cemetery on the West Bank. In 1860, his remains were moved to the Green Mount Cemetery in Baltimore, Maryland.

The inscription on the bust of McDonogh reads: "Remember labor is one of the conditions of our existence."

Soldier of Three Wars

The statue of a soldier atop the tall, imposing pedestal now located at Poydras and Loyola was originally located at Canal and Claiborne. Construction of I–10 necessitated its being relocated. The statue represents men who fought in the Spanish-American War, the Philippines Insurrection, and the China Expedition.

It has been jokingly said, "Now it stands on guard, overlooking the Howard Johnson hotel, to be sure there is not a recurrence of the 1973 sniper incident." This is possibly why he has his rifle in a ready position to help at a second's notice if needed.

General Albert Pike

This statue was also located at the intersection of Canal and Claiborne. When I–10 came through, it was necessary to move it to its new location at the intersection of Tulane Avenue and South Jefferson Davis Parkway.

Pike was an Episcopal bishop. When the Civil War broke out, he laid down his religious cloth for the sword.

Edward Douglas White

This statue was originally located in front of the old Civil Courts Building in the 400 block of Royal Street. When the Civic Center opened, the statue was moved in front of the Louisiana Supreme Court Building on Loyola Avenue. The statue also received a new pedestal, compliments of the lawyers of Louisiana.

The inscription on the base of the monument tells of White's career as an associate justice of the Louisiana Supreme Court, a United States senator, and finally, chief justice of the United States Supreme Court.

Not a bad record for a boy from the bayous of Lafourche who, up until he served as a private in the Army of the Confederate States of America during the Civil War, had never left his native state.

Henry Clay

Clay was truly a great American statesman and a renowned and highly respected orator. His statue was originally located in the center of the neutral ground on Canal

Edgar Douglas White

Henry Clay

Street between Royal and St. Charles. Because of the traffic congestion caused by the statue's location, in 1900 it was
decided to move it to the center of Lafayette Square
(bumping Benjamin Franklin from this prestigious spot).

There are three statues in Lafayette Square—John
McDonogh, Benjamin Franklin, and Henry Clay—but
none of General Lafayette. There is only a small brass
plaque that tells us that a magnolia tree was dedicated to
the memory of General Lafayette.

Benjamin Franklin

This statue has moved four times, and is ready to move
again.

In 1844, American sculptor Herman Powers, then working in Florence, Italy, received $1,000 as partial payment
of his fee for a statue of Benjamin Franklin. The money
was sent him by Richard Henry Wilde, who represented a
group of New Orleanians. When the Civil War started, the
statue was still not completed. Wilde died in 1867, and
because of the calamity of the war, the statue was totally
forgotten until 1869.

In time, a member of the committee contacted Powers.
He apologized for the delay. He advised the committee
that he would complete the statue, and at the same time,
because of the inconvenience he caused, waive the balance
due him.

The statue arrived in 1871, but was unclaimed and was
advertised for sale by mistake. The mistake, thankfully,
was corrected before the statue fell into someone else's
hands. The base was ordered from Boston, and, as luck
would have it, the ship carrying it sank. Finally, the needed
base for the statue arrived. It, along with the statue of
Benjamin Franklin, was installed in the center of Lafayette
Square. When Henry Clay's statue was removed from Canal Street (see page 138), it was decided that because of the
affection of New Orleanians for Clay, he should have center stage in Lafayette Square. Therefore, Franklin's base

Benjamin Franklin

Mother Seton

and statue were moved to the Camp Street side of the square. It has been said that because of the shabby treatment he received from the city's political leaders, his statue was placed with his back facing City Hall in defiance.

By 1909, the Italian marble of the Franklin statue began to deteriorate. It was decided it should be moved indoors into the recently completed New Orleans Public Library. When that building was demolished, the figure was set up on the campus of the Benjamin Franklin Senior High School. With a new Benjamin Franklin Senior High School under construction, it looks like another move is about to come.

Yes, there is a statue today of Benjamin Franklin in Lafayette Square facing Camp Street. In 1926, Henry Wadsworth Gustine, a native of Chicago who spent his winters in New Orleans, donated a second statue of Franklin to be placed where the original stood.

This magnificent statue—the second one—survived yet another great movement to have it removed. During World War II, General Allison Owen, then president of the Parkway Commission, recommended the statue be the first to be melted down if military needs dictated such a drastic move. Owen stated, "It's bronze and a poor work of art. Anyhow, Franklin never had the direct connection with New Orleans that Henry Clay or John McDonogh had."

As in his lifetime, Benjamin Franklin was bigger than life, and a survivor. Although pushed around a lot in our city, he is still larger than life and still standing in Lafayette Square, as well as at Benjamin Franklin High School.

Mother Seton

Mother Seton was the founder of the Daughters of Charity in North America. She was also the first saint canonized in North America by the Catholic church. The beautiful statue of Mother Seton originally stood in front of the Hotel Dieu Hospital on Tulane Avenue. The old hospital was torn down and a new one built. Mother Seton was moved, and today stands in front of the new Hotel Dieu Hospital located on Perdido Street.

Grecian Cup Bearer

When the Delgado Museum of Art in City Park was dedicated, a beautiful statue of the Grecian cup bearer, Hebe, was proudly placed in a pool of water in front of the museum. In time, and without moving an inch, the Grecian cup bearer found herself standing in front of the New Orleans Museum of Art. The name "Delgado Museum of Art" was removed and replaced with the name "New Orleans Museum of Art."

In 1977, Hebe was evicted from the spot she had occupied for close to fifty years. Her original spot today is filled with a modern-day mobile sculpture. Hebe was moved to a spot in the rear of the museum. Several years later, yet another move, her third, came about, and today she stands in the park's greenhouse. Like the song says, "That ain't no way to treat a lady. . . ."

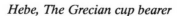

Hebe, The Grecian cup bearer

*The New Orleans Cotton Exchange Building (*New Orleans--The Crescent City *by George W. Engelhardt)*

(Courtesy of City Park)

Bare-Breasted Maidens

In the 1920s, the old New Orleans Cotton Exchange Building on the corner of Carondelet and Gravier streets was torn down. It was considered the most ornate building in the city in its heyday. When constructed in the 1800s, it cost $380,000 and was the talk of the town.

Before the structure was demolished, the statues of five large bare-breasted maidens were carefully removed. The voluptuous statues, all five of them, made their way to City Park. As visitors to the park drove down Lelong and Anseman avenues, reactions to seeing them for the first time were mixed. The five statues were larger than life size. Seen at ground level for the first time, they were awesome. Some who saw them were in shock, with frowns on their brows. Others were delighted, and it showed by the smiles on their faces and a twinkle in their eyes. The frowns must have outnumbered the smiles, or their owners possibly were more vocal, for the controversial statues were removed from the park.

Two of the statues made their way to 116 City Park Avenue, then headquarters of Weiblen Marble and Granite Company, and now the home of the Firemen's Charitable Benevolent Association. Just as the two voluptuous ladies greeted visitors at the front door of the New Orleans Cotton Exchange in the 1800s, today they greet the visitors at the front door of the Firemen's Charitable Benevolent Association.

The remaining three statues, as of this writing, have not been located.

Unfortunate Boot

In ninety-one years, five statues and five different locations.

In 1898, the statue of a young boy in jeans holding a boot up to examine a hole through which water flowed into a pond in which he was standing was dedicated at the

Milliken Children's Hospital of Charity. This was one of the country's earliest children's hospitals. This popular statue remained there until the hospital was torn down in 1930. A new Charity Hospital had just been built on Tulane Avenue, and the statue was moved to the reflecting pool in front of the hospital. In 1961, the statue was vandalized. The only thing left that was recognizable was the boot, which today decorates the hospital administrator's office.

In 1920, Mr. and Mrs. William Frazer Owen donated to City Park a copy of the ever-popular statue. A pool and fountain were built on the City Park Avenue side of the park, where the statue was placed. The statue, fountain, and pool were donated in memory of the premature death of the Owens' young son. In 1929, the statue broke, was removed, and sent to be repaired or replaced if not repairable. Inspection showed that repairs were not possible. A new 400-pound replica—statue number three—was sent to the park. Upon its arrival, New Orleans multi-millionaire oilman and member of the City Park Board, William McFadden, objected, as he had just given his wife a similar bronze statue—statue number four—which was installed in their garden adjacent to the park. McFadden was most generous to the park, and a champion of many of its causes. The board of directors, in their infinite wisdom, voted to heed McFadden's wishes. In place of the popular "Unfortunate Boot" statue, a statue of "Chloe" took the spot once occupied by the boy with a hole in his boot.

Upon Mr. and Mrs. McFadden's death, their property became part of the City Park complex; today Christian Brothers School occupies the McFadden home. The statue of the unfortunate boot, like the words in the song "These boots are made for walking," took a hike. It is no longer on the grounds at City Park or the Christian Brothers School.

After close to sixty years the boy in the jeans, holding a

boot in his hands with water flowing through the hole—
statue number five—has found his way back to New Orleans. This time he is proudly standing in a pool at Children's Hospital. He still has that bewildered look on his
face, saying to himself, "Where is all this water coming
from?"

Over the past ninety-one years this statue has occupied
space at three hospitals and a park, as well as the grounds
of a private home. Who knows, the hole may have been
caused by the numerous moves thus far made.

The Goddess of History

John James Audubon

Goddess of History and Alcee Fortier

In 1884–85, New Orleans hosted a World's Fair-World Industrial and Cotton Exposition. The grounds of the fair were previously the home of Louisiana historian Charles Gayarre. A statue of the goddess of history was displayed on the World's Fair grounds in his honor.

Another Louisiana historian of note was Alcee Fortier. He was also honored with a statue placed on the grounds of the fair. When the fair closed, both statues were moved. The statue of the goddess of history—called for many years "the mystery monument" (see page 62)—is located in a small triangular park named in honor of Charles Gayarre. This park is at the intersection of Esplanade Avenue, Tonti Street, and Bayou Road. The whereabouts of Fortier's statue is still a mystery.

John Audubon

The last of our moving statues is located in the park that bears his name: Audubon. Just as he moved from place to place in his lifetime, devoted to painting birds, so too has he moved from one spot to another in Audubon Park. At first, the statue was located close to Magazine Street. When the zoo underwent a monumental overhaul, Audubon was hauled to a new location, and now stands in the confines of the zoo area, close to Monkey Hill. The statue of John J. Audubon, considered the most important monument in the park, depicts Audubon in his familiar stance—with paper in hand, ready to do what he did best, which was drawing pictures of birds. The inscription on the statue reads:

John James Audubon
Of Louisiana
Naturalist and Ornithologist
Author of the "Birds of America"
1780–1831

WE HONOR THE LADIES

Many good ladies of New Orleans played an important part in the city's colorful history. Some of them, rightfully so, have been immortalized in statues made of exotic materials such as bronze, granite and marble. One has even been covered with a very expensive gold leaf. On the other extreme, one is made of that inexpensive material, cement.

Margaret Haughery

New Orleans proudly boasts of having dedicated the first statue of a female in the United States. The year was 1884, and the recipient of the honor was a loving and compassionate Irish lady named Margaret Gaffney Haughery. Although she was illiterate and had suffered great losses in her lifetime—her husband and only child died just two months apart—Margaret, without the benefit of any education, but with great determination, dedicated her life to serving others.

She helped build virtually every charitable institution caring for orphans in the city. She also built a highly successful bakery and dairy business. When she died, she stipulated in her will, which she signed with an "X," that all of what she had amassed in her lifetime be given to the charities she supported.

Because of her years of untiring work with orphaned children, her statue shows her with a child at her side. There is no flowery epitaph to read. The only word on her monument is "Margaret." It was said she was a living example of charity; she gave without expecting anything in return.

Molly Marine

Another first in America in the feminine statue department is that of Molly Marine. Molly proudly stands in her marine uniform on the corner of Canal and Elks Place.

Margaret Haughery

Molly Marine

The statue was dedicated in 1943 during World War II. This statue was the first of a female service woman in the United States. The model for the statue was Judy Mosgrove, who still resides in New Orleans.

The statue is unique in the fact that it is made of cement. It was wartime and that was the only material available. The legend on her pedestal tells the story of what she was all about: "FREE A MARINE TO FIGHT."

In 1966, a group of ex-marines financed a beauty treatment for Molly. She received a coating of bronze and a new marble pedestal. One might wonder if she received a new Maidenform bra at the same time!

Mother Cabrini and Mother Seton

Two religious statues that have gained attention and generated controversy are Mother Frances Xavier Cabrini and Mother Elizabeth Seton.

Mother Cabrini

The statue of "Mother Cabrini," as she was affectionately called, is located on the neutral ground at Harrison Avenue and Canal Boulevard. It was a gift to the city from the Order of Alhambra.

No sooner was the religious statue dedicated than some people objected vehemently to the statue of a religious figure on city-owned property. Hearings were held to listen to both sides of the issue. The people of the city recalled the great works of the saintly woman, a native of Italy, who was a tireless and fearless worker for the needy of the city of New Orleans.

After hearing all sides, Louis H. Yarrut, a Jewish judge, ruled the statue would remain, and a rare endorsement was presented on a plaque that was placed beneath the inscription of the Order of Alhambra.

> Accepted by the City of New Orleans in grateful appreciation of the outstanding civic worth of Mother Frances Xavier Cabrini.

NOTE: Please see page 142 for the story of Mother Elizabeth Seton.

More Bare-Breasted Maidens

Other female statues that caused commotion are located in the fountain pool in front of the New Orleans Lakefront Airport. These ladies, besides being totally nude, are enormously buxom. When dedicated, they created heated controversy that lasted for some time. Like the cool water in the fountain in which they stand, the furor cooled off in time. Today they go almost unnoticed.

Joan of Arc

Although not a citizen of New Orleans, she is honored in New Orleans just the same. The reason has to do with the fact that Orleans, France, in 1429, was a city on the verge of falling into the hands of the much-hated English.

Joan of Arc

Sophie Bell Wright

Joan, without the benefit of schooling, especially military training, was nonetheless very bright and persuasive, with an over-abundance of shrewd common sense. When she was only thirteen, she heard "voices," and saw visions of her favorite saints and angels. When the siege of Orleans began, the voices told Joan to go to Orleans and lift the siege.

In answer to the voices, she assumed the masculine dress of a page. Upon arriving in Orleans, she was so convincing in her discussion with those in charge, she was given complete command of a force of troops. Without the aid of strategy or military tactics, she simply used her good common sense. Because of this, along with her all-impelling inspiration, the French troops fought fearlessly against overwhelming odds and were victorious in saving the city of Orleans—the sister city of New Orleans.

Although she was victorious in fighting the overwhelming odds of the army of England, she was a loser in fighting a much smaller but well-organized political force which had her put on trial as a heretic. On May 31, 1431, just two years after her glorious victory that saved the city of Orleans, she was burned at the stake in Rouen, France.

She instantly became a martyr of the church. Her flaming death inspired the French people to the unification and final expulsion of the feudal division that had existed for centuries. As a reminder to the French people of Joan's ultimate sacrifice, there is a beautiful statue of Joan burning at the stake located in Rouen, France. In 1920, 491 years after her death, she was finally canonized by Pope Benedict XV.

Here in New Orleans, dedicated in 1984 as a reminder of her exploits to all who live here, is a beautiful statue showing Joan in her military clothes, mounted on her horse, rallying her troops to save Orleans, France, from its conquerors.

For her glorious efforts, the statue of Joan of Arc in New Orleans is laminated with 4.5 percent gold leaf. May it shine for at least 491 more years as a reminder of this great lady's achievement and sacrifice.

Sophie Bell Wright
1866–1912

Just as the Margaret Haughery statue was the first statue dedicated to a female in the United States, the statue of Sophie Bell Wright is the last statue to be added to the seemingly endless list of statues in New Orleans. Just as Margaret Haughery gave to her fellow man more than she received, the same is true of Sophie Bell Wright. Like Margaret Haughery, she had a difficult time as a young person, but was able to overcome all obstacles.

From an impoverished family, and crippled from a fall at age three, Sophie's bright outlook on life never faltered. As a very young girl, she opened her first school in her mother's parlor. At age fourteen, she started a private school for girls called Home Institute. When she was twenty, she started the city's first free night school. Boys who were forced by circumstances to work during the day could receive their education no other way. Multitudes are indebted to her for this innovative approach to education.

Sophie's entire life was one of giving. We hope the larger-than-life bronze statue reminds all who see it of this phenomenal nineteenth-century educator. She overcame all seemingly insurmountable obstacles. Sophie's simple formula for success was desire, dedication and determination, coupled with persistence and a proper attitude. It allowed her, in spite of her handicaps, both physical and financial, to become one of the leading nineteenth-century educators in not only New Orleans but the entire United States.

Over the years, the statues of the goddess of history, Margaret, Molly, Hebe, Joan, Mother Cabrini, Mother Seton, Chloe, Sophie, and the multitudes of bare-breasted maidens who have never been given names, have all given us much pride, enjoyment, and, in some instances, controversy.

It would be unforgivable if this section on statues of females were completed without mention of a great lady named Angela Gregory. No, Angela is not immortalized in statuary form. But she will always be remembered as the great New Orleans sculptress, who in 1955 unveiled a five-ton bronze statue of Bienville, the founder of New Orleans, which she designed and produced.

U.S. EQUESTRIAN STATUES

The position of the horse's front hooves tell the fate of the rider.

Left foot lifted—killed in action or died from wounds received in battle.

General Albert Sidney Johnson (Metairie Cemetery). Killed on very first day of Battle of Shiloh.

Right foot lifted—expired normally.

General Pierre Gustave Toutant Beauregard (entrance to City Park). Confederate officer who fired the opening cannon shot of the great drama at Fort Sumter. After the Civil War, he built a railroad, ran a lottery, and was once mentioned as a candidate for emperor of Mexico. He died in 1893 at age seventy-five.

Both front hooves lifted—rider went on to greater glory.

General Andrew Jackson (Jackson Square). Savior of the city of New Orleans and first Southerner elected President of the United States.

Mardi Gras

PARADE CITY, U.S.A.

New Orleanians' addiction for parading is unequalled, not only in the United States, but anywhere in the world. Parades have been recorded in the Crescent City as early as July of 1734, when the good sisters of the Ursuline Order dedicated their first convent.

True, the largest number of parades is during the Carnival season and Mardi Gras, but parades for every occasion are spread throughout the year. There are parades for the Sugar Bowl, St. Patrick's Day and St. Joseph's Day, for the Spring Fiesta, and at Christmastime, to name just a few. Throughout the year, jazz funerals take to the streets carrying to their final resting places those who have contributed to this world-renowned music that was born in New Orleans in the early twentieth century.

The following tongue-in-cheek story is in reference to New Orleanians and their love of parades. When New Orleans was a very young city, a man was convicted of some supposedly heinous crime. He was sentenced to be hung by his legs in the Place d'Armes (now Jackson Square), where the local citizens could pass and scoff at him.

The sentence was carried out as ordered, with two guards posted beside him at all times. After many, many hours of hanging in this most uncomfortable position, with a continuous flow of angry people passing, one of the guards heard the man mumbling faintly. He leaned over and heard the man singing very softly, "I love a parade." It seems that New Orleans' love of parades has never diminished and apparently never will.

HARD TO EXPLAIN

Mardi Gras, more so than any other New Orleans historical subject, is the most difficult to explain to people who have never witnessed the celebration firsthand. The main reason for the difficulty is the fact that Mardi Gras is a participatory celebration, not one you just go witness. Once you attend one Mardi Gras and become infatuated with it—and almost everyone who attends for the first time does—your first inclination is to tell your friends who have not attended what it is like. It is then you find out it is a most difficult task to accomplish.

Be that as it may, let us try, as best we can, to share with you the difference between Carnival and Mardi Gras, how the dates are determined, why we throw trinkets from the floats, what the colors stand for, and how the "anthem" of Mardi Gras was born. This chapter will also cover the coldest Mardi Gras, years the celebration was cancelled and why, where the first Mardi Gras parade was held in North America, an unusual marching club, the tradition of breaking the glass once Rex has toasted his queen, the story of the ever popular king cake, and the year real royalty bowed to New Orleans' Mardi Gras make-believe royalty.

THE DIFFERENCE BETWEEN
CARNIVAL AND MARDI GRAS

Carnival is a season of merriment starting on January 6, King's Day—or, if you prefer, "Twelfth Night" (twelve nights after Christmas). It was on this day the three wise men visited the Christ child. The Carnival season in New Orleans officially begins with the ball of the Twelfth Night Revelers, the second-oldest Carnival club (1870) in New Orleans.

Mardi Gras is a French term. Its translation is "Fat Tuesday," the final day of celebration, when the Christians can get their fill of merriment and food and libation before the forty days of Lent begin.

HOW DATE IS SELECTED

Mardi Gras has fluctuating dates that can fall between February 3 and March 9. The reason for the various dates stems from the fluctuating dates of Easter, determined by Pope Gregory the Great, the same man who gave the world the calendar we all use. It is called the Gregorian Calendar. Pope Gregory determined the date of Easter, the greatest of all Christian celebrations, using a formula based on the paschal full moon. As Easter was the greatest of the Christian feasts, the date was selected so the full moon would allow Christians who had to travel long distances to the major cities to do so by the light of the full moon.

For a list of Mardi Gras dates, past and future, see *Mardi Gras and Bacchus: Something Old, Something New*, by Gaspar J. ("Buddy") Stall, also published by Pelican.

THROWS, MUSIC, AND COLORS

Throws

Mardi Gras is a Christian festival borrowed from the pagans. The pagans who survived the dreaded winter showed their appreciation to their gods by throwing flour (the symbol of life) into the fields.

Maskers on Mardi Gras floats throw to the crowds in appreciation for coming to witness the parade. Before there were parades in New Orleans, the old pagan custom of throwing flour was practiced, but got out of hand and was banned by law.

Music

His Imperial Highness, Alexis Romanoff Alexandrovitch, Grand Duke of the Russian Empire, was touring the United States in late 1871 and early 1872. He attended a musical comedy entitled "Bluebeard," in which the lead

was sung by Miss Lydia Thompson. In the play, she sang an absurd ballad called "If Ever I Cease to Love." The Grand Duke became infatuated with both the song and Lydia and followed her on her tour that ended in New Orleans. Rex was formed that year and held its first Mardi Gras parade in honor of the Grand Duke. To please him, the song "If Ever I Cease to Love" was played for him and was adopted as the official song of Mardi Gras.

Colors

In 1872, when Rex organized their first parade, there was not sufficient time to make a costume, so a costume was borrowed from Lawrence Barrett, a local actor who was playing the part of Henry III at the Variety Theater. His cloak was purple, with rhinestones as green as the sea, and his scepter and crown were gold; hence the colors of Mardi Gras were born.

In 1892, the Rex parade theme was symbolism of colors, with purple representing justice, green for faith, and gold for power.

COLDEST DAY EVER RECORDED

The coldest temperature ever recorded in New Orleans was on February 14, 1899. Along with the all-time low temperature of 6.8 degrees Fahrenheit, snow and sleet were also falling. Oh, yes, the day also happened to be Mardi Gras.

Approximately a week prior to Mardi Gras, with each day's temperature breaking previous lows, people started to panic. They were concerned as to whether Rex would cancel their parade. Their anxieties were calmed when Rex put a proclamation in the newspaper several days prior to Mardi Gras. It stated that the parade would roll as usual, provided the good people cleared the parade route of snow and sleet in front of their homes. The people responded, and so did Rex.

Bright and early Mardi Gras morning, Walter Denegre, Rex that year, was at the den readying himself for the exhilarating ride ahead. He fortified his insides with ample antifreeze. He also protected his outsides with layers of thermal underwear. He looked quite chubby in his royal regalia, but his body was as warm as toast.

Exactly on time, Rex, while still in the den, mounted his float. When the giant doors swung open, it was as though the curtain had been raised on a great theatrical production, and a grateful and appreciative crowd applauded vigorously. It was a most unusual sound, for the clapping was muffled by the gloves worn by the crowd. The king of Mardi Gras, to show his appreciation, greeted his subjects with a smile. Because of the extreme weather conditions, smiling for the entire parade proved to be the easiest thing he did all day—for the smile on his face was simply frozen.

With temperatures of 6.8 degrees Fahrenheit, and snow and sleet, the Rex parade that year proved, if nothing else, that Mardi Gras is truly show business, and the show must go on.

YEARS MARDI GRAS WAS CANCELLED AND WHY

Beginning in 1805 through 1823, all Mardi Gras balls were cancelled because of man's inhumanity to man. This is to say that the animosity between the Americans and Creoles was such that it was not a good idea to get them together in the same place.

1806 through 1827, all Mardi Gras outdoor masking was cancelled for much the same reasons. The maskers had begun throwing stones instead of sweetmeats and handfuls of lime instead of flour, etc.

1862–1865—War Between the States

1875—political unrest

1918–1919—World War I

1943–1945—World War II

1951—Korean War

1979—New Orleans police strike

Since organizing in 1872, the Rex parade has been cancelled due to rain only once—in 1933.

ST. LOUIS CEMETERY MARCHERS CLUB

As steeped in history as the New Orleans cemeteries are, it was not only natural but expected that they would somehow get involved in the Mardi Gras celebration, and get involved they did.

In 1911, a novel group entitled "The St. Louis Cemetery Marchers Club" was formed. This colorful krewe was made up of those involved in the Good Government League movement. Their objective was to eliminate from the voting rolls those who were already residents of the local cemeteries—some of whom had been there long enough to return to dust.

For good reason, members of this new group kept their identities secret. Although it was difficult, with great determination they were able to secure a funeral hearse. As

Mardi Gras approached, some of the members got cold feet and dropped out. Others, with a sense of dedication when taking on a project, continued their plans for the Mardi Gras burlesque.

The big day, February 28, arrived and all were ready. The masked krewe members were chomping at the bit to bring their political message to the crowd. At the forefront was the one and only float (a glass-enclosed jet black funeral hearse), entitled "Medicine," which depicted life and death. The driver wore a black costume and death mask, and beside him was Beelzebub, holding a banner with skull and crossbones. Inside the hearse was a ballot box and a skeleton seated in a coffin. Around the skeleton's neck was a sign that read "Dead, but still a voter."

Those following the hearse wore death masks and white sheets to cover their bodies and white hoods to cover their heads. The walking members represented the Graveyard Pleasure Club, Girod Cemetery Voters League, and the Tombstone Brigade. They carried signs that read "Count me in for several votes," "I'll be with you on election day," and "How often will I vote next year?"

When this colorful group met the Mardi Gras crowds, the people followed them like moths being drawn to a fire. They were pleased as punch with the response. Although they were somewhat burlesque in their approach, they were dead serious (forgive the pun) in their aim.

At an appropriate spot, they joined in and followed the tail end of the Rex parade, to the delight of the crowds. One spectator watched as the silent parade passed and remarked, "Their silent message is more meaningful than any spoken word I can imagine." Unfortunately, the Police Inspector heard of their escapade and sent word requesting that they discontinue their march before reaching City Hall. With their goal being one of fair play at the voting polls, they decided to adhere to the wishes of the Inspector and disbanded shortly before reaching City Hall.

The member costumed as the skeleton inside the funeral hearse during the parade was a prominent judge who, a short time after Mardi Gras, revealed his identity upon leaving his legal chambers. He was the Honorable Judge Edouard F. Henriques. Other members of this long-remembered group were influential doctors and other highly respected citizens of the city of New Orleans.

KING CAKE AND FIRST CLUB
TO USE SAME

Thanks to the pagans, the king cake (originally called "king's cake") became a part of the Christian celebration. The Christian church offset the abominable and intolerable pagan celebration with one that was toned down, yet still enjoyable and tolerable. The pagans selected as their king a young man who, as king of their celebration, received anything and everything he so desired for a full year. Of course, when you receive you must pay. The pagan king's cost was a supreme price to pay for being king for one year, for at the end of his reign he became a human sacrifice.

The Christian church toned this barbaric practice down considerably. A "king's cake" was baked with a bean inside. Whoever received the slice with the bean became the king of the celebration.

This tradition has been part of the New Orleans celebration from almost the beginning, and has reached its greatest popularity at the present time. In recent years, enough king cakes, now prepared with a plastic baby in place of a bean, have been produced to allow the city to almost double its population each and every year during Carnival and Mardi Gras. It is estimated that close to one half million are sold and consumed each year during the Carnival season and Mardi Gras. Entrepreneurs have been able to expand the king cake's popularity and now ship them throughout the United States and to every corner of the globe.

Since January 6, 1870, when the Twelfth Night Revelers held their first Carnival ball, they have used the king cake as a means of selecting their queen. Unfortunately, the court fools who were to serve the ladies of the court at that first celebration were intoxicated, some spilling the cake on the ladies' laps, and others, who were more than a little drunk, throwing cake at them. To say the least, the ladies were horrified and stunned. They showed their displeasure in the following manner: the lady who received the piece with the bean swallowed it in contempt. The bean acted like a birth control pill, for there was no queen "born" in 1870. The following year, the court fools were better behaved, and Mrs. Emma Butler proudly acknowledged receiving the golden bean, making her the very first queen of a Carnival ball in the Crescent City.

The Twelfth Night Revelers still use this means of selecting their queen at the ball. The one difference is that today

a giant, wooden, beautifully decorated cake, with small drawers in it, is used in place of a real cake. Each of the maids pulls out a drawer (similar to a wedding cake pull done in New Orleans). The one receiving the golden bean is the queen of the ball.

A few last words about the very popular king cake. The reason so many are sold in the metropolitan New Orleans area lies in the fact that almost every school classroom, thousands of business offices, and thousands of families participate in buying the king cake, whereby a winner is selected whose duty it is to buy the next king cake.

During the Great Depression, when things were so bad financially, some people got married just to get the rice. Children were told when going to a king cake party that if they happened to get the slice with the bean in it, to not hesitate to swallow it. If you didn't, you would have a lot of explaining to do to your mother when you got home.

OFFICIAL AND UNOFFICIAL
END OF MARDI GRAS

Just as there is an official beginning of the Carnival season that starts on January 6, there is also an official ending of Mardi Gras. Just prior to midnight on Mardi

Gras, Rex's officers and royalty join Comus and his queen at their ball. Rex and Comus escort each other's queens in a grand march. At the end of the march, and at the appropriate time, Rex waves his scepter, officially bringing Mardi Gras to an end for another year.

At approximately the same time, an unofficial ending of Mardi Gras takes place in the French Quarter. This one is on Bourbon Street. The wall-to-wall carpet of humanity is dispersed by the men in blue, mounted on horseback, as they slowly walk down Bourbon Street in a wedge configuration. Following the mounted police are water trucks with powerful water jets, washing the trash to one side, followed by street sweepers with powerful mechanically-driven brushes sweeping up the trash. Behind them are empty trucks, followed by men from the parish prison, picking up the tons and tons of trash and placing it in the empty vehicles. The efficiency and precision with which the French Quarter is cleaned and cleared is almost as entertaining and colorful as any Carnival or Mardi Gras parade.

LENT BEGINS

With the long Carnival season and Mardi Gras celebration over, it is hoped that all Christians are sufficiently filled with merriment, food, and drink to last the forty

days of Lent. To help prepare them for this time, approximately one hundred balls, and between sixty and seventy street parades, are held for the enjoyment of the masses. Each year, the celebration gets larger in hopes it will make the Lenten period more tolerable.

Since the fourth century, Christians have carried out the ritual of going to church on Ash Wednesday and standing before their priest, who, using his thumb, makes the sign of the cross on their foreheads (with ashes made by burning the palms from the previous Palm Sunday services). As the priest makes the sign of the cross, he says, "Remember, man, from dust thou came and to dust thou shall return."

MARDI GRAS TRIVIA

Mayor and King

Since the very first Rex parade in 1872, only one New Orleans Mayor, Joseph A. Shakespeare (1882), served as king of Mardi Gras.

Queen of Comus and Rex

In the history of Mardi Gras only one lady, Mrs. Emily Hayne, served as both the queen of Rex (1923) and Comus (1925).

New Orleans—Royal Wedding

In 117 years, only one king of Mardi Gras (Rex) married his queen.

In 1895, Frank T. Howard (one of five immediate members of his family to gain royal honors from Rex) married his queen, Lydia Fairchild.

Mardi Gras Floats

Mardi Gras floats have traveled the streets of New Orleans since the first Comus parade rolled with only two floats on February 24, 1857. Early Mardi Gras floats were

small, with just a few masked riders. More recent floats are much larger, with up to seventy-five to eighty masked riders. This year super floats will be introduced by the Krewe of Endymion, and will carry over one hundred masked riders.

The sizes, designs, and modes of propulsion for Mardi Gras floats have changed over the years. One aspect that has not changed since throws became an integral part of Mardi Gras parades has been the similarity between the Mardi Gras floats of the streets of New Orleans and ships of the oceans. Just as a ship cuts through the water, lifting waves as it passes, Mardi Gras floats cut through the sea of humanity, lifting a wave of arms until they pass.

New Orleans' Largest Parade Float

With New Orleans being the Mardi Gras capital of the world, you would assume that a Mardi Gras parade would contain the largest float.

WRONG!

On April 12, 1860, a parade was held in honor of the unveiling of the statue of the popular Henry Clay. The statue was located on the neutral ground on Canal Street between Royal Street and St. Charles Street. The parade had only one float, but it was a whopper and a half. A fifty-ton, three-masted sailing ship was taken out of the waters of the Mississippi River, placed on an undercarriage, and pulled by a team of horses down Canal Street, around the statue, and back to the river. As the ship moved down Canal Street, sailors raised and lowered the sails to the rhythm of the nautical music of the band that led the parade.

Louisiana's First Mardi Gras Celebration

The first Mardi Gras celebration in Louisiana took place on the banks of the Mississippi on March 3, 1699. This was the day that Iberville discovered the mouth of the Mississippi River. He camped out that same evening, and since it was Mardi Gras, they had a celebration. Iberville named this spot Point d'Mardi Gras, and the small bayou adjacent to it Bayou d'Mardi Gras. These were the first names on the Louisiana map other than the Indian names.

The First Mardi Gras Parade in North America

The first Mardi Gras parade in North America using floats, costumed riders, and flambeaux was the Comus parade of March 24, 1857.

First Rex Parade

The Krewe of Rex was conceived of and implemented its first parade in only ten days. It did not have sufficient time to build floats. Therefore, the first Rex, Mr. Louis J. Salomon, rode a horse.

Rex at the 1885 World's Fair (Courtesy of New Orleans Museum of Art)

Doubloons

The first Mardi Gras doubloon was introduced to Mardi Gras with the Krewe of Rex. In 1884–85 New Orleans hosted a World's Fair. The main building covered thirty-three acres—enough area to hold four Louisiana Superdomes. Rex traditionally arrived in New Orleans by way of the river on his royal yacht on the Monday before Mardi Gras. In 1885, he visited the main building of the World's Fair. To commemorate the occurrence, a doubloon showing the Rex coat of arms on one side and the 1884–85 World's Fair main building on the other side was struck.

Oldest Marching Club

The oldest Mardi Gras marching club is the Jefferson City Buzzards. They were founded in 1889 and chartered in 1890. At one time in their colorful history, the club marched black-faced. Although that tradition has been discontinued, the club is still very active and one of the highlights of Mardi Gras in the Crescent City.

The Buzzards start early on Mardi Gras, and go full speed until Mardi Gras officially ends. They have been known to partake of the spirits during the course of the festivities. One member said he was sad because one month after last year's Mardi Gras, one of his marching buddies passed away. He said he was also happy because when they carried out his buddy's written request to be cremated, his alcoholic content allowed him to burn all the way through to this year's festivities!

Mardi Gras and Christmas

December 25 was looked forward to by a small select group of young New Orleans socialites, and not only because it was the birthday of Christ. Awakening bright and early Christmas morning without the need of an alarm clock was not a difficult task. It was on this day the young ladies of the social register anxiously awaited a visit from royalty in the form of a duke of a Mardi Gras krewe whose job it was to deliver boxes of flowers containing a dozen red, long-stemmed American Beauty roses.

When the duke arrived and presented the box of flowers, the young maiden's heart rate increased substantially, and her hands trembled. With great anticipation, she unwrapped the box and searched through the roses to find the much-cherished parchment scroll that announced whether she would be a maid of the krewe's upcoming Mardi Gras ball, or be summoned to serve as queen of the Mardi Gras festivities.

The young maiden, on Christmas morning, with the Christmas decorations of red and green surrounding her, had visions not of sugar plums dancing in her head, but of a crown signifying her as queen.

Zulu

The first Mardi Gras club founded by the black citizens of New Orleans is the Zulu Social Aid and Pleasure Club, or simply "Zulu." In 1909, the members of a social club called the Tramps attended a play. The highlight of the evening was a skit entitled "There Never Was and There Never Will Be a King Like Me." The members of the Tramps were so impressed with what they had seen that they reorganized, and in 1910 held their first Mardi Gras parade. The Zulus were officially incorporated on September 26, 1916.

The club did not have a great deal of money, so the Zulu king, William Story, wore a costume made of sack material that had pictures from tobacco cans and cigarette packs on it. On his head he wore a silver lard can cut to look like a crown. As a scepter he used a banana stalk. This was symbolic, for he worked as a longshoreman carrying bananas on the riverfront. Since he did not have a royal yacht to carry him to the city, he came up the New Basin Canal in a rowboat.

At one time, the second float in the Zulu parade was a flatbed wagon with a wood stove, men cleaning catfish, and a woman frying the fish. When the Zulu king saw a pretty girl in the crowd, he pointed his scepter at her. The Zulu police would carry her to the Zulu float, lift her up, and the king would give her a warm, soft kiss. He would then send her to the second float, where she received a hot mouthful of tender catfish. What more could a girl want on Mardi Gras?!

Trucks

Decorated trucks with masked riders have been a part of Mardi Gras since the early 1900s. The photo shown is one of the earliest trucks.

(Courtesy of the Louisiana State Library)

MAY 1989

MARDI GRAS - 1990

New Orleanians—Diehard Paradegoers

It has been said that the people of New Orleans love Carnival and Mardi Gras parades to such an extreme that if a catastrophe were to occur and only two people survived, at the next Mardi Gras one of them would be in costume marching down the street beating a drum and holding a banner, while the other would be standing on the side in costume, drinking a Dixie beer and hollering, "Throw me something, mister!"

Rex Toasts His Queen

Each and every Mardi Gras, the royal float of Rex comes to a halt in front of the Boston Club located on Canal Street. Rex lifts his glass, toasts his beautiful queen, and then throws the glass to the pavement below. The tinkle of the breaking champagne glass below the royal throne is the echo of a tradition which originated long before our

New Orleans Mardi Gras was born. This ancient custom, transferred to our make-believe royalty, originated from the thought that after a toast to the king's beloved or favorite, the drinking vessel should never again be used for something less noble. This and many other traditions, some borrowed from the past and some conceived by our Carnival krewes, make the New Orleans Mardi Gras unlike any other Mardi Gras celebration in the world.

Real Royalty Bows to Make-Believe Royalty

Mardi Gras 1950 will long be remembered by Reuben H. Brown and Mary Brooks Soule. As king and queen of the Mardi Gras, they were doubly honored, for in attendance during their reign were none other than the Duke of Windsor (former king of England Edward VIII) and his Duchess.

Arrangements were made for the Duke and Duchess to review the Rex parade from the Boston Club gallery along with the Carnival queen and her court. After the parade, which the Duchess described as "fabulous," and then added, "and such fun," cocktails were served at the Beauregard House, followed by a most elegant dinner at Antoine's.

At approximately 10 P.M., the royal couple arrived at the Municipal Auditorium. Concern now climaxed as to what would happen when the royal couple were presented to the Carnival rulers, Comus and Rex. It was Mardi Gras custom for all gentlemen to bow and all ladies to curtsy when presented to the Mardi Gras king and queen. All anxieties withered away when the real royal duke bowed low and the duchess presented a most royal and elegant curtsy to both Comus and Rex and their queens.

Needless to say, the people of New Orleans were bowled over by the good sportsmanship of the royal visitors. As the British would no doubt put it, "They were jolly good sports."

CHAPTER 7

Truth is Sometimes Stranger than Fiction

GENERAL JAMES WILKINSON

General James Wilkinson (the man for whom Wilkinson Street, one block long in the French Quarter, is named) was a very colorful and controversial figure to say the least. He fought brilliantly with Generals Washington and Benedict Arnold in the Revolutionary War. He was such a gifted military tactician and politician that he received the star of a brigadier general at the tender age of twenty. Even though he received it at this age, he didn't get to keep it very long. It was learned he had plotted to oust General Washington as Commander-in-Chief. This was only a temporary setback for this cunning and controversial man. Like a boomerang, he came back, rising to the position of commander of the U.S. Army.

On April 30, 1801, Wilkinson issued the first regulation on hair length in the annals of the U.S. Army. From that day forth, soldiers were required to keep their hair closely cropped. He was most emphatic in seeing that no soldier wore a "queue," a lock of hair resembling the ponytail of today. He said the queue was useless and expensive, as well as unhealthy. The truth is Wilkinson did it for political reasons. Those who wore this style of headdress were flaunting their anti-Jeffersonian politics. By passing this regulation, he demonstrated his loyalty to the new president, Thomas Jefferson.

Almost all military men of all ranks adhered to the new regulations. The lone dissenter was Lt. Col. Thomas Butler, who declared the order "an arbitrary infraction of my natural rights." He vehemently refused to have the offending hair cut. Because he was an aged, experienced, highly decorated officer, who had gained the respect of influential people during his years in the army, Wilkinson chose not to challenge him.

In January of 1803, the straw that broke the camel's back fell when Wilkinson ordered Butler to a new post, and the insubordinate Butler, already standing on thin ice, refused to go. This time Wilkinson would do more than just blow off steam to cool his temper.

On June 1, 1803, he ordered Butler to stand trial. The charges were two-fold: refusing to cut his hair and refusing to proceed to his new post. Influential Andrew Jackson interceded on Butler's behalf. Jackson stated at the trial, "Sir . . . the golden moment . . . when all the Western Hemisphere rejoices at the joyful news of the cession of Louisiana . . . we hope will not be . . . marred by the scene of an aged and meritorious officer . . . before a court martial for the disobedience of an order to deprive him of the gift of nature . . . worn by him both for ornament and convenience . . . " With Jackson's support, Butler received a mild reprimand as punishment, and was directed to obey the two orders he had refused to follow. Shortly after the trial, Butler was assigned to a new post in New Orleans, an order which he carried out. Perhaps because of the mild

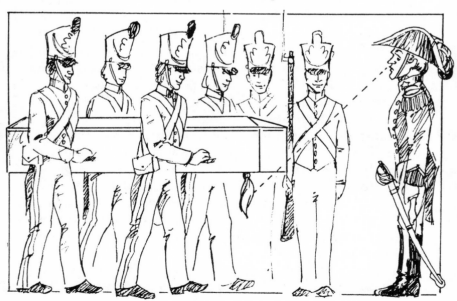

reprimand he had received, he decided to keep the haircut that started the rift with his superior. When Wilkinson learned that Butler had still not removed the offending queue, he scheduled a new trial in New Orleans for July 1, 1805. He now had his adversary just where he wanted him. This time there would be no leniency. Butler had no influential friends in New Orleans to come to his aid. Wilkinson was right. With a speedy trial, Butler was found guilty. He was sentenced to a suspension of "command, pay, and emoluments" for a full year. When the sentence was carried out, his hair style would be carried out with it.

As the old saying goes, "He who laughs last laughs loudest," and Butler did get the last laugh, even though it was a silent one. Before the sentence could be carried out and Butler disgraced, he learned he had contracted yellow fever and the end was near. As his last request, knowing full well that the entire garrison, including General Wilkinson, would attend his funeral, Butler issued the following directions for his burial: "Bore a hole in my coffin under my head and let my queue hang through it, that the damned rascal may see that even when dead I refuse to obey his order." His final request was carried out as directed. Even though a funeral is normally a solemn occasion, this one, no doubt, had more chuckles than sobs.

A WHAT JUST HIT YOUR HOUSE?

On February 19, 1921, seventy-three-year-old Mrs. Stenhouse, of 317 Alix Street in Algiers, was on the receiving end of a prank that took place across the river from her home. Late that night, an unidentified person climbed the picket fence in front of the Presbytere. With him he carried gunpowder and a four-inch iron ball. The reason was that on display in the arcade in front of the Presbytere was a Civil War cannon. The prankster loaded the cannon with the powder and cannonball. He then looked around to be

sure he was not being watched. As soon as the coast was clear, he fired the charge.

The concussion knocked down the night watchman, and it broke sixty windows in buildings in the area. Shortly after leaving the barrel, the ball struck and bent one of the iron pickets of the fence in front of it. The cannonball, at a high velocity, went screaming over Jackson Square, narrowly missing the bronze head of General Andrew Jackson.

Its final destination was the second-floor bedroom of Mrs. Stenhouse. She was knocked onto the floor by the concussion from the cannonball landing in her bed. The room immediately filled with thick dust from the plaster walls, which were totally destroyed by the shot.

Mrs. Stenhouse was bruised a little and shaken, but otherwise unharmed. Mrs. Richard J. Stenhouse, daughter-in-law of Mrs. Stenhouse, called the police after she attended to her mother-in-law. When they answered, she frantically repeated, "A cannonball has just hit our house!"

The policeman replied, "A what?"

"A real cannonball. I heard it screaming just before it crashed into my mother-in-law's bedroom. It was still warm when I picked it up."

"Lady," said the policeman, "are you sure someone is not full of home brew?"

After a quick investigation, the police found that the shot was real and the damage was real. To remove temptation from other would-be practical jokers, the muzzles of all cannons on display around Jackson Square were filled with concrete.

The statue of Andrew Jackson in Jackson Square today is a representation of him on his horse holding his hat in his right hand. Had the shot fired on February 19, 1921, been a little lower, he would not have a head to put his hat on.

NEW ORLEANS' FIRST FOOTBALL GAME

College football today bears no resemblance to the first Princeton vs. Rutgers game of November 6, 1869. With twenty-five men on each side, the game began with a kick of the ball to the quarterback (hence the name football). A combination of soccer, prize fighting, pushing, and shoving followed, resulting in plays lasting up to five minutes.

On January 1, 1890, at Sportsman Park, New Orleanians witnessed their first football game, held on that date because college students were home for the holidays from schools in the East. It was a benefit game, one team representing Princeton and the other side Yale. Adding color to the game, the referee wore a tall silk hat.

Following is the flourishing description of the game in the January 2, 1890, *Picayune*:

> Yesterday, fairness nowhere appeared to better advantage than upon the broad green field at Sportsman Park with sturdy, picturesque oaks at the far end and the grandstand filled with the choicest flowers of New Orleans' society.
>
> The game lasted less than 45 minutes with a score of 0 to 0. The game ended abruptly because of an overenthusiastic kick that sent the city's only football spinning into the New Basin Canal, where with a ruptured bladder it slowly sank out of sight.

NEW ORLEANS' FIRST
PROFESSIONAL FOOTBALL GAME,
OR, DRAMA IN THE PRESS BOX

New Orleans promoter C. C. Pyle signed a contract with the world champion Chicago Bears to play an exhibition game in New Orleans on January 10, 1926. Pyle felt success was guaranteed because the Chicago Bears was the hottest team in football at that time. They also had on their roster the first certified pro football superstar, Red Grange (better known to the sporting world as "The Galloping Ghost"). Pyle agreed to pay Tulane's assistant football coach, Lester Lautenschlaeger (called the Little Dutchman when he quarterbacked the Tulane football team), $6,000 for expenses to put together a team of Southern All-Stars, including himself, to play the Bears.

The day before the game, knowing of Pyle's rotten reputation for fulfilling his financial obligations, Lester demanded and received $3,000 cash, with an agreement the balance would be paid at halftime at the game. The game was played before a large crowd at Old Heinemann Park, located at the corner of Carrollton Avenue and Bienville

Street. At halftime, quarterback Lester Lautenschlaeger went looking for Pyle and the $3,000 owed the team, but neither was to be found.

Lester, instead of going to the locker room, quietly and calmly went straight to the press box and sat down. When puzzled sportswriters asked him what he was doing there, he told them that if he didn't get the $3,000 owed the team, there would be no second half. Word of what was transpiring found its way to Pyle, who rushed to the press box and demanded Lautenschlaeger and his teammates get down onto the field and play. Lester again very calmly and quietly told Pyle to give him the $3,000 owed the team and they would gladly finish the game. Pyle came up with the $3,000 in cash and the game was completed.

After the game was over (Bears 14, Southern All-Stars 0), the money was divided among the Southern All-Stars who had participated in New Orleans' first professional football game, which offered drama both on the field and in the press box.

When the officials of Tulane University (who frowned on professional football) found out that Lautenschlaeger had played in the game, his contract was terminated.

Dynamic men always overcome adversities. Lautenschlaeger was no exception. In 1927, he once again walked on the sidelines in Tulane Stadium as an assistant coach. In 1935, he was offered the top job at his alma mater, but for personal reasons graciously refused.

SMOKEY MARY

The Pontchartrain Railroad that ran from the river to the lake down Elysian Fields Avenue in New Orleans began operation in 1831. On the day the dedication was to take place, the steam engine, built in Europe, had not arrived, but the dedication took place just the same. Mules

were used to pull the railroad cars from the river to the lake, loaded with political leaders and other dignitaries.

When the engine finally arrived, it did not have sufficient power, so sails were added to supply the additional power needed. The little engine belched smoke profusely and covered the passengers, who rode in open cars; hence, the nickname "Smokey Mary" stuck until the line was discontinued.

HISTORY'S MOST UNFORGETTABLE CRAWFISH

The tale of the most expensive crawfish to dig its way into Louisiana history, you'll no doubt agree, is unusual, but it is a true one.

Out of necessity, all plantation owners on the lower Mississippi, for their physical and financial protection, had around-the-clock levee watches. The most feared word of all plantation owners was the word "crevasse," which means "break in the levee" and instant trouble. But even

with this type of precaution, there was still trouble to be found.

In the spring of 1912, the Louisiana sugarcane crop promised to yield an all-time Louisiana high. The 1911 crop was excellent, and back-to-back high-yield crops could mean instant financial success and possibly even becoming a millionaire.

On May 14, 1912, at exactly 6:30 P.M., on the levee thirty miles upriver from New Orleans at the Hymelia Plantation, an undetected crawfish hole suddenly erupted into a crevasse. This crawfish hole was only one-and-a-half inches in diameter, but penetrated extremely deeply, and resulted in hydraulic pressure which forced the river water into the air fifty to one hundred feet.

When Mr. Emile Borch, owner of the plantation, was summoned to the site, his lower jaw fell almost to his knees, for he knew instantly that all was lost.

Within a half-hour, the small crawfish hole had grown into a break in the levee fifty feet wide, and like a cancer continued to spread and bring with it total devastation.

Even though Mr. Lorio, a member of the Levee Board and owner of a nearby sawmill, had his logging train, men, and equipment on the scene pronto, by 9 A.M. the next morning the crevasse had grown to 900 feet across and was still growing.

The Army Engineers had now arrived, and after a quick assessment of the situation, without hesitation estimated that it would cost $150,000 to close the gap. Their first question was, "Who is to pay the bill?" A heated argument erupted between Mr. Borch and the members of the U.S. Corps of Engineers, and was stopped only when a messenger delivered a telegram from the president of the Mississippi River Commission. It read, "Hold end of crevasse. Do not attempt to close until the commission meets next Thursday."

Remember that all of this time an estimated three million gallons of river water per minute were turning Mr. Emile Borch's magnificent plantation into a soggy, marshy swamp where the crawfish would be the only ones to profit.

One can only wonder if anyone ever had the audacity to ask Mr. Borch if he cared to come over for a crawfish dinner.

LAST PUBLIC EXECUTION—
END OF 19TH CENTURY

Public hangings in New Orleans were commonplace for many years. They were held in various places, such as Place d' Armes, Congo Square, at the corner of Orleans and Rampart, and on the neutral ground in front of the parish prison on Orleans Street. The beginning of the end of public hangings came about because of the following ugly incident.

Two New Orleans men named Delisle and Adams murdered a woman for what they believed to be a bag of jewels, only to find out the bag contained pecans. They were captured, tried, found guilty, and sentenced to hang. They were placed in Parish Prison until the sentence could be carried out.

On the date of their hangings, in spite of horrible weather conditions, a multitude of curious onlookers were on hand. The two men were brought to the gallows that were set up on the neutral ground in front of the prison. As they were brought out of the jail, the weather got progressively worse. The sky grew dark and gloomy, angry flashes of lightning lit up the scene, followed by the dull, rolling noise of light thunder in the distance. When all was ready, the hangman's nooses were placed around the necks of the two men.

Adams, without any emotion, accepted the fate that was before him, but Delisle became violent and demonstrative. Several guards subdued him and the rope was finally placed around his neck. With the two men now standing on the trapdoor, and a light, dreary drizzle falling, the trapdoor opened.

At that very instant, a bolt of lightning struck, blinding the crowd. This was followed instantly by a clap of deafening thunder that almost frightened the crowd into spasms. Rain followed in torrents, drenching all in attendance. Many were so frightened they fled the scene. When the fear, which was only momentary with most of those present, had somewhat subsided, the ropes were seen dangling and swaying loosely in the wind, for the lightning had struck them. The bodies of the two men were on the pavement below the gallows. Delisle was apprehended when he tried to crawl away. Adams's arm was broken. He was in severe pain.

Pity for the two men became predominant in the hearts of the multitude, but the law was inexorable, and its servants were compelled to perform their unpleasant duties for a second time. Without hesitation, the two men were picked up and brought back to their former positions on

the trapdoor. New ropes were put into place as the heavy rain soaked Delisle's and Adams's trembling bodies. The crowd, now horror-stricken and feeling pity for the two criminals, requested leniency, but without hesitation the two were hung.

The Delisle-Adams hangings were the last public hangings in New Orleans, for their hangings were viewed with so much abhorrence and indignation throughout the city that the legislature at the next session passed a law prohibiting public executions.

LAWS OF THE PAST

Without laws to govern us, life for the most part would be intolerable. This does not mean, by any stretch of the imagination, that all laws are fair. To the contrary, over the years, New Orleans has adopted many that were unfair, some that were unusual, even unbelievable, and yes, some that were humorous. The following are some examples.

Riverfront

Prior to there being warehouses on the riverfront to protect freight from the elements, a colonial law was instituted with the hopes of cutting down on theft by assisting police during the dark nights, and read as follows: "The wheels of all carts shall remain ungreased so that they may scream and thereby produce an automatic alarm

for the ears of the revenue officers." Years after the American occupation, the carts in New Orleans were still screaming obedience to the old law that had long been discontinued.

Thieves, being the cunning people they are, soon found a solution to the above. They would go below the wharves in boats, and from there they would bore holes through the wooden floors of the warehouse into the sacks of coffee, flour, beans, and whatever else was in the warehouse. The plunder would then fall into the boats, and the thieves would make off like the bandits they were.

Homefront

One of the strangest laws ever found existed during the Spanish regime between 1762 and 1803. If a woman was accused of being unfaithful to her husband, she and the man charged, along with her husband, were brought before a judge. The judge heard the case, and if he found them to be guilty, the husband was allowed to pass sentence. He was told by the judge, "Remember whatever you decide to administer as punishment will be given not only

to the man but to your wife as well." No doubt these were chauvinistic times, for there was no law with reference to unfaithful husbands.

Aviation

By the mid–1930s, aviation in New Orleans had progressed to the point that young aviators were looking for new challenges to show their skills and bravery. Just upriver on the east side above the newly constructed Huey Long Bridge was located an air strip. The bold young pilots using this strip began showing their skills and bravery by flying under the bridge.

Before long, this feat was a piece of cake. They then started doing loop-the-loops around the bridge. The officials were quick to pass a law stating it was unlawful to fly under the Huey Long Bridge. The reason was that it was feared that if one of the planes crashed into the structure, the gasoline would ignite the wooden railroad ties, and the intense heat generated, with no way of extinguishing the fire, would possibly cause the steel structure to collapse.

Headdress

New Orleans quadroons (one quarter Negro blood) were considered by many writers to be some of the most beautiful women in the world. The Caucasian ladies of New Orleans knew of the hanky-panky going on between these beautiful women and the white male aristocrats. They especially disliked the quadroons flaunting their beauty, latest fashions, hairstyles, and gorgeous hats, by riding in chauffeur-driven carriages around the French Quarter. In order to fight back, the Creole ladies had an ordinance passed which stated that all black females were required to wear a *tignon* (a turban-like, brightly colored madras handkerchief) at all times.

After the law was passed and enforced, writers wrote that it appeared that the law had not achieved its goal, for the *tignon* required to be worn by all women of color framed the quadroons' faces and made them even more beautiful.

Parks

It seems that people are always finding ways to abuse good things. In the 1800s, public squares were not being used for what they were meant to be. Instead, women started to clean their rugs in the public squares. To put a stop to this unsightly practice, a law was passed making it illegal to clean rugs in public parks.

Horses

A law was passed in the 1800s making it a crime when attempting to sell a horse to place a small linen bag filled with red pepper with vinegar under the horse's tail. This would make the animal hold his head up high, stick his ears forward, lift his feet with agility, and caper about like a young colt. This did not allow a true evaluation of the animal and, therefore, was unfair and unlawful. Again, these were biased times, for the law only applied to animals, not people.

Bizarre Law

Louisiana, in its illustrious history, has had many strange and sometimes unbelievable laws. None were any stranger or more unbelievable in their enforcement than the one outlined in the following recorded incident.

In the winter of 1765, Jean Baptiste, a slave of Sieur Robin deLogny, committed suicide by hanging himself from the limb of a peach tree. The superior council met and agreed that proper justice had to be carried out as prescribed by the statute making it unlawful to commit this hideous crime. The unusual case began, with prosecution of the corpse taking place immediately. A curator was appointed, and the owner of the slave was interrogated at great length. After this, the body was viewed by one of the council and the curator.

Upon completion of this gruesome trial, the commission judge stated that, "The whole council solemnly adjudge the defendant guilty of the infamous crime of suicide. . . . "

As punishment, the council "condemned his memory and perpetuity," and ordered the public executioner to tie the corpse to a frame on the back of a cart, head downward and face to the ground, and to drag it through the

streets of New Orleans to a place where it was hung by the feet from a scaffold for twenty-four hours, after which it was thrown in the "public sewer" (the river?).

This case proved that truth is sometimes stranger than fiction.

LONGEST PRIZE FIGHT ON RECORD

On April 6, 1893, in the hot, humid climate of New Orleans, Jack Burke and Andy Bowen, both displaying superhuman physical endurance, engaged in the Lightweight Championship of the South prize fight, which ended to the liking of neither fighter. After battling for an unbelievable and unforgettable record-setting 110 rounds that lasted seven hours and nineteen minutes, each man was totally drained of all his energy and unable to continue. The fight ended in a draw, meaning that neither man received any money. The rules at that time stated that the winner would take all. Since neither one could continue, all they received for their record-breaking performance were totally drained and equally bruised and bloodied bodies.

NEW ORLEANS' MUSICAL EARTHQUAKE

Although New Orleans is in a sense earthquake free, it did have an unusual one that made the front pages of newspapers across the country.

In December 1884, the opening ceremonies of the New Orleans World's Fair were held in the auditorium of the main building. It was a monstrous room, seating 18,000 with no obstructions. The world's largest organ was installed to fill this great hall with sound.

At the very end of March, 1885, the German specialist who built and installed the organ thought he could get better results if he raised the organ pipes to come within six inches of the roof. He felt the roof would act as a sounding board and distribute the sound more evenly. Late in the evening, when the great hall was unoccupied, he stationed men in all corners of the giant auditorium and told them that once he started to play to raise their arms as soon as sound reached them, and to keep them up, thereby signifying that the sound quality had improved.

He started off by playing a waltz. Almost immediately, every arm raised in unison and remained up throughout the entire composition. The German was so pleased he broke into a spirited John Philip Sousa march. The volume of sound coming from the pipes proceeded to make the thick roof boards go up and down as if they marched to the tune. The final result was that the roof came tumbling down.

On April 1, 1885, newspaper headlines across the country read, "New Orleans Suffers Musical Earthquake." Although the date was April 1, this was not an April Fools' joke.

IT SURE SEEMS HOTTER THAN IT USED TO BE!

New Orleans is one of the few places in the world where artificial changes in its natural physical conditions have been extensive enough to change the temperature of the overlying atmosphere.

This deduction was made by Dr. I. M. Cline, internationally noted meteorologist who served as the chief of the U.S. Weather Bureau in New Orleans for over thirty years. His statistical data covered fifteen years prior to and after the city's sub-surface drainage system was installed in 1900.

Cline's statistics pointed out that from 1885 to 1899, New Orleans had never reported one hundred degrees, but from 1900 to 1914, one hundred degrees and over temperatures were recorded approximately 50 percent of those years. From 1885 to 1899, ninety-five degrees or higher was recorded only thirty-five days, and from 1900

to 1914, seventy-four days of ninety-five degrees or higher were recorded. It was also noted that the average daily temperatures were higher.

The cause of this phenomenon was simply the installation of sub-surface drainage that drastically reduced the level of the water table in the city. Water in the drainage canals was lowered in 1900 by eight to ten feet. Dry land is heated much more rapidly by solar radiation than water is. Equal quantities of heat acting on equal areas of land and water increase the temperature of the land nearly twice as fast as they do the temperature of the water. Yes, the new sub-surface drainage kept rain water out of our streets and homes, but in turn put beads of perspiration on our brows, our backs, and all over our bodies because of higher temperatures.

Like the TV commercial says, "It's not nice to fool Mother Nature."

TEACHER EXTRAORDINAIRE

As a young boy in Germany, Carl Cramer was gifted with a magnificent singing voice. As an opera singer he was outstanding and won national acclaim. As successful as his career was, his love was not opera, but two other artistic fields, painting and sculpture. With God-given talent, excellent training, and total dedication, he mastered both.

In the 1950s, Carl came to New Orleans by way of New York. He began selling his paintings and sculptures to varied clients, not only in New Orleans, but throughout the United States. His reputation became widespread and his list of clients grew. Just as he had gained national fame as an opera singer in Germany, he gained national fame in the United States as a painter and sculptor.

As a man with deep compassion, Carl many years ago ventured on a unique project that had others snickering under their breath. How could he possibly teach sculpture to blind students of all ages? He did it through unmatched talent, patience, and total commitment. For years he has taught blind students to do busts of themselves, with phenomenal results. Students who live a life of darkness receive a new spark of life given to them by the master.

Carl beams with pride when speaking of one of his students who, after serving many years as a nurse at the Carville leprosy center, lost her eyesight. With no previous training as a sculptor, or even knowledge of her hidden talents, she enrolled in Carl's class and not only finished, but was so talented that she, without the benefit of sight, now teaches sculpture to students at Carville who have sight.

POSSIBLE RELIEF TURNS
INTO QUICK DISBELIEF

Because of their city's hot and humid climate, New Orleanians no doubt became ecstatic when they found out in the early 1800s that relief was finally on its way. A sailing ship was headed for New Orleans loaded to the gunwales with ice taken from the frozen lakes of Maine.

Upon its arrival, a large crowd gathered at the levee. Their great excitement was unfortunately short-lived. As soon as the ship was moored, New Orleans mayor Augustine McCarty, with a police escort, went on board. The mayor quickly told the cheering citizens, "As your duly elected mayor, my duty compels me to protect you even though what I am about to do will be unpopular." He then ordered the police to throw the ice overboard.

The crowd quickly went from cheers to sneers. In unison, the irate mob demanded to know why he had done such a dastardly deed. The mayor quickly responded, "The city's medical supervisor has advised me that medical scientists believe a cold substance taken into the human body will induce tuberculosis." The crowd's response no doubt was "bah, humbug." The first shipload of ice that was to have brought possible relief had only brought disbelief.

STRANGE, BUT IT WORKED

One of the unusual as well as crude customs in regards to food in the old days (before store-bought baby pacifiers) was as follows:

A mother would tie one end of a string around a piece of pork and the other end to her baby's foot. If the baby happened to choke on the piece of pork, his kicking movements would jerk on the string and pull out the homemade "pacifier."

As stated, it was strange, but it was also very effective.

PETE GREETS THE POPE

New Orleans' own Pete Fountain is proud as a peacock for having been selected to play his famous tune, "A Closer Walk With Thee," during the mass celebrated by

Pope John Paul II on his visit to New Orleans in 1987.

Pete, with great anticipation, was all decked out in his tuxedo and ready to leave. As he reached the front door, his wife, Beverly, mentioned that the weather looked threatening and that it might be a good idea to take an umbrella along. Pete's granddaughter gave him her yellow umbrella and asked him to use it because it was the color of the day. There would be yellow and white flags and yellow flowers, and the yellow umbrella would fit right in. Being an obedient grandfather, Pete smiled and took the umbrella.

Beverly was correct in her evaluation of the weather. Standing on stage in the rain under the yellow umbrella and looking over the hundreds of thousands of people in front of him, Pete and the crowd watched as the pope paraded in his famous popemobile. When the pope arrived at the altar site he looked to his left in the direction of Pete.

Pete immediately sensed both the crowd and the pope staring at him with big smiles on their faces. Pete looked up; his face turned a deep red when he realized what the crowd and the pope were smiling at. Pete, in his fancy tuxedo and with clarinet in hand, was standing under a yellow Donald Duck umbrella.

The pope probably thought to himself, "He plays beautifully, but he sure has a strange sense of humor."

CHAPTER 8

Storyville

SHADY PEOPLE/SHAKY BEGINNING

A young boy, around seven years of age, was standing in front of a house of ill repute. A lady, seeing him and knowing the nature of the house, asked him what he was doing standing there. "Waiting for my mother," was his friendly reply. She was shocked. With horror and condemnation on her face, she partly covered her mouth with one hand and blurted out, "Your mother is a prostitute?" "No ma'am," he replied, "she's a substitute—only works on Mondays, Wednesdays and Fridays."

This chapter, as you may have surmised from the above story, covers the oldest profession in the world, prostitution. To understand how and why Storyville, which consisted of thirty-nine square blocks of legal prostitution, came about, let us take a look at the deplorable conditions leading up to the days of Storyville.

New Orleans, like every port city in the world, has had its share of problems in this specific area. In 1718, Jean Baptiste le Moyne Bienville, the founder, set foot for the first time in what is now called New Orleans. The majority of his party were brought to do the dirty work of clearing the land, building houses, etc., etc. Most of these men were salt smugglers from the jails of France.

That same year the king sent a second boatload of people. Included on the list of 189 people were seven tobacco smugglers, three dealers in contraband salt, six vagabonds from Orleans, ten vagabonds from Lyons, twenty women taken for fraud, and sixteen women from the Rockford House of Correction in France. You can see from the manifest that the scum of France had been sent.

Many of the females who arrived were prostitutes. This was, of course, not unusual for the time. It was common practice for the crown to send prostitutes to the areas where soldiers were sent to fight and where explorers opened new territories. Louis XIV and in particular Louis XV, through his regent, the Duke of Orleans, in a manner of speaking could be considered the city's first procurers.

In 1721, yet another shipload of females was sent to Louisiana. This one carried eighty prostitutes from LaSalpé-triére House of Correction in Paris. For many years, a large percentage of the female population in New Orleans was from the wrong side of the tracks.

A visiting journalist many years ago wrote that after researching the early years of New Orleans, with the original group containing so many males from the jails of France, followed by boatload after boatload of females from houses of correction, he highly recommended that people shy away from tracing their ancestry to the beginnings of the city. He went on to say he could almost guarantee they would turn up relatives they would rather not know about. He went on to say, with tongue in cheek, that the union of these two unsavory groups might go a long way towards explaining Louisiana politics and politicians.

It is hard to believe, but things did get worse before they got better. John Law, the Scottish promoter whose scheme it was to build a city called New Orleans for the king of France, had committed to having a certain number of people in Louisiana within a given time period. He painted a rosy picture of the city. His promotion claimed the river water was as clean as crystal, fish were bountiful, game was as plentiful as sand on a beach, and there was more tasty food than could be consumed by the heartiest of appetites. He went so far as to advertise precious gems lying on the bare ground. All one needed to do was bend over and pick them up. His cornucopia was not only loaded to the fullest, but was literally running over.

What people did find when they got here were not the items advertised, but lots of alligators, mosquitos, and snakes. Word eventually got back to Europe, and no one wanted to make Louisiana their destination. But Law had a quota to fill and quickly found a simple solution. He had two laws passed that solved his quota problem. One stated that anyone in jail, no matter what the crime, was set free provided they went to Louisiana. Secondly, anyone out of work for three consecutive days was sent to Louisiana. Prostitution was not considered a legal profession, therefore, in the early years many of those sent to New Orleans were lewd and abandoned women from the streets of Paris and other towns and cities throughout France.

The early years of New Orleans were truly stormy ones filled with unsavory characters. That the city survived at all was truly a miracle. Besides the less than desirable quality of people, the city was located below sea level, with no levees to hold the river back when the snow in the North melted. But not only did the city survive, in time it even thrived.

THE GOLDEN ERA

With the invention of the steamboat in 1812, New Orleans was about to enter its golden era. History teaches that where there is great prosperity there will always be large numbers of prostitutes close behind. Prostitution and prosperity were both at their zeniths during the golden era. When ships came into port, boatloads of girls were taken to the ships even before they docked. They were appropriately labeled "the Boat Girls."

The most unusual of the city's prostitutes were appropriately labeled "the Mattress Girls." These girls, unable to find any kind of employment, even in houses of ill repute, as a last means of survival actually walked the streets with mattresses on their backs. When they found a client, well, you get the idea.

These girls were considered unfair competition by those who worked in the brothels; therefore, they had to be eradicated. The solution used was rather simple. When the street walkers found a client, unrolled their mattresses, and went to work, the other women simply waited for an opportune moment and then threw buckets of water, sometimes very hot water, on the Mattress Girls and their clients.

LICENSE FOR LEWD
AND ABANDONED WOMEN

By 1856, citizens and a large number of religious groups were literally up to their armpits in the social and economic problems caused by prostitution, which ran rampant throughout the city. Something had to be done. It was suggested that an attempt be made to regulate it legislatively.

After a short study, an ordinance was written and presented to the city council. In 1857, ordinance 3267 was passed. This was the city's first ordinance to acknowledge the existence of prostitution. It required women in this profession to be taxed in the form of a license that cost $300.00. It was also the first attempt at regulating prostitution in the U.S. Unfortunately, it was short-lived, for it did not survive its first legal test.

The madams were not going to take this new attempt at controlling them lying down (no pun intended). They joined forces and agreed that their group would purchase the license and then challenge it in court.

On May 22, 1857, Mrs. Emma Pickett purchased a license to operate a brothel at 25 St. John Street. Upon receiving it, she filed suit against its constitutionality, and the case went to court. In 1859, the ordinance was declared by law to be unconstitutional. All women who purchased the license prior to the ruling were given back their money plus interest.

When reading the license (see above) please note, on license number nineteen, that May Baily could work only at 423 Dauphine Street on any floor except the ground floor. This was added to keep from having a recurrence of what had happened previously when women literally dragged men off the street. It was also explained that because only so much money could be extracted from clients for sexual pleasure, the first floor was always used for drinking and gambling. This way most or even all of a man's money could be spent before leaving.

THE SWAMP, GALLATIN STREET, AND SMOKY ROW

The Swamp

A notorious section of the city, where sin ran rampant, was called "the Swamp." The area was bounded by S. Liberty, S. Robertson, Girod, and Julia Streets. The Swamp was made up of cheap dance halls, brothels, gambling halls, and saloons. All of the buildings were one story high. Between 1820 and 1850, over 800 known murders were committed in this small area appropriately labeled "Hell on Earth."

Gallatin Street

As bad as the Swamp was, Gallatin Street, although only two blocks long, was even worse. Gallatin Street (no longer in existence) was located in the French Quarter directly behind the U.S. Mint, where the flea market operates today. A policeman who was foolish enough to enter Gallatin Street alone to handle a complaint became either a casualty or a missing person. Police quickly learned to handle complaints on Gallatin Street only in well-armed, organized groups, and only in the daytime.

Some of the toughest people, both men and women, made Gallatin Street their headquarters. For example, America Williams, "the world's strongest whore," along with fugitives from every part of the world, found shelter on Gallatin Street. It was so tough that it was considered a miracle if a man entered with money in his pockets, visited each bar, and left Gallatin Street still alive and with money in his pocket. Gallatin Street was considered around the world as the toughest street on the face of the earth. It was called "the port of missing men."

The street was named for Albert Gallatin, secretary of the treasury in the cabinet of Thomas Jefferson. He must have been a beloved man all over the country, for there were mountains, lakes, rivers, and towns named in his honor. Apparently in New Orleans he was considered a scoundrel, for the locals named the toughest and dirtiest street in the world in his honor.

Smoky Row

Another virtual cesspool of sin was called "Smoky Row." It was even smaller than Gallatin Street, being only one block long. It was located on Burgundy Street between Conti and Bienville. Nearly one hundred black women of every imaginable age lined the banquettes day and night waiting for customers. If a prospective customer did not show any interest, it was not uncommon for the women to spit tobacco juice into his eyes, blinding him temporarily. While incapacitated, he was hit over the head with a bat, dragged into an alleyway, robbed, and thrown back into the street. In 1886, things had gotten so out of hand throughout the French Quarter that an ordinance was passed requiring the strumpets not only on Burgundy Street, but also Customhouse (now Iberville), Bienville, Dauphine, St. Louis, and Conti to vacate the ground floors. Most of those who were displaced from these areas relocated on Franklin Street.

Conditions by the late 1800s had worsened to the point that there was believed to be at least one house of ill repute in every block in the city. Prostitution had infiltrated even the better neighborhoods. The *Mascot* newspaper blatantly featured stories and pictures of lesbianism, houses of prostitution in the better neighborhoods, secret sessions of the city council at houses of ill repute, and unregulated employment agencies whose main purpose was to obtain children for careers of sin.

Once again, drastic situations required drastic measures. Something had to be done. Intolerable conditions existed and unless checked would eventually devour the entire city. Property values were going down, down, down. If necessary, even a major compromise would be considered by the area conservatives to stop the spread of prostitution. A Society for the Prevention of Cruelty to Children was formed and headed by the Reverend Alfred E. Clay. It helped, but was far from solving the overall problem.

BEGINNING OF STORYVILLE

The man of the hour in this time of need was Alderman Sidney Story. He was a highly successful businessman and a respected citizen. He loved classical music and deplored the music we today call jazz. He also detested the level to which New Orleans had sunk.

Story spent a great deal of time planning a solution to the problem. Once his preparations were completed, his plan was put into action. He solicited and received the aid of a very capable New Orleans attorney named Thomas McCaleb Hyman. Story knew that all previous legislative attempts had been shot down by the courts. He was confident that Hyman could, if given sufficient time, write an ordinance worded in such a way that it would be acceptable.

While Hyman was working, Story went on an extensive tour of port cities throughout Europe. The purpose of this

was to see just how they were able to control the problems of prostitution. With all the research done and Hyman's carefully worded ordinance polished to the teeth, Story presented his ordinance to the city council. The city council passed the new attempt at controlling prostitution on January 29, 1897. The ordinance limited prostitution to the area between N. Robertson and N. Basin, and from Customhouse to St. Louis Street.

Attempts were made to modify the ordinance by adding two additional areas of the city, one downtown and one uptown. This never came to pass. A try at destroying the ordinance was put into effect on September 22, 1897. A homeowner, George L'Hote, whose residence was one half block from the area designated, and the Church Extension Society of the Methodist Episcopal Church, whose building was in the area, jointly filed suit against the Story ordinance. (It was later reported that the women who worked in the house of ill repute next to the church would tell the men upon leaving the church, "Now that you have heard about heaven, come over here and let us show you what heaven on earth is like.") The case went all the way to the highest court in the land, the United States Supreme Court, which affirmed the constitutionality of the Story ordinance.

Others who opposed it vehemently were landowners who made large sums of money renting houses to the madams in every part of the city. The New Orleans medical profession was also in opposition to police-supervised medical examinations for prostitutes. New Orleans also had a small army of gonorrhea doctors who advertised quick cures for the venereal diseases. They saw the end of their free ride coming with the ordinance. Some of the city's most popular madams were also opposed to being herded into one area designated by the city fathers. Some left, but most returned at a later date.

Alderman Sidney Story was the man who carried the banner of righteousness and respectability, bringing New

Orleans' uncontrolled vice to an abrupt end. Day after day, more and more houses outside the area stood dark and empty. The plan was a huge success from the very beginning. For the first time in New Orleans' history, the runaway, uncontrollable prostitution had the reins put on it successfully. Mr. Story was aghast when he found out the local press had given the area the nickname "Storyville."

CHARACTERS OF STORYVILLE

Storyville, to put it mildly, was a lively place. What made it so above all other things were the characters who worked there. It would be impossible to cover all of them in just one chapter of a book, so let us get a close look at just a few.

Joe the Whipper

Joe the Whipper was living proof that there were many different ways of making a living. Joe made a very comfortable living in a most unconventional way. His working day consisted of making the rounds to the many whorehouses of the district. That, of course, was not unusual, for many different vendors made rounds to the various whorehouses every day. What made him unusual was that upon arrival he administered beatings to masochistic whores.

The women had a choice of whips, leather straps, canes, switches, and even steel rods. Joe was said to be a very accommodating fellow. If a special request was made he always fulfilled that request, no matter how bizarre it might be. You can bet that over the years there were many weird and unbelievable requests that made his job a challenge each and every day.

Because of the nutty nature of his work, Joe may have been the first to use a slogan still used today: "service with a smile."

Tom Anderson—Super Pimp, Louisiana State Legislator, and Mayor of Storyville

Irishman Tom Anderson made his first sound in New Orleans in 1858 when slapped on the bottom by the doctor to start his life. In spite of being born into poverty, and in spite of his total lack of formal education, he was never slapped around by anyone again in his life.

As a very young child he became a hawker for the *Daily Picayune*. He soon learned that a great deal more money was available as a trusted stool pigeon. He aided the police department and himself in this manner. He maintained the newspaper job as a front for his more profitable position as a stoolie.

Tom Anderson

Before long he had a third income, delivering cocaine and opium to local prostitutes. All of this entrepreneurship and he had not yet reached his teen years. As a young man astute with figures, a talent which was self-taught, he became a bookkeeper for the Louisiana lottery.

This job was too tame for Tom. He knew the benefits of working for himself. He was a wheeler and dealer and therefore opened a restaurant. Many contacts with the police, politicians, and prostitutes, based on his past dependability, blessed him with a large patronage. Once the restaurant was on sound footing, he opened another, plus several saloons.

Tom was a superior businessman. For reasons unknown, he was drawn to the seedy side of business. With all his other entrepreneurship he still found time to invest in and foster several houses of ill repute. Money was pouring in by the barrels-full. In spite of his known illegitimate businesses, he was elected to the Louisiana state legislature, where he served for sixteen years. What better place to use his wheeler-dealer talents?

It was during this period that he went into the oil business. In a short time he owned or partly owned three large oil companies. Serving on many important state committees, he was really in the driver's seat. His legitimate businesses, with his political contacts, were growing as fast as his illegitimate businesses. At the right time, he sold his oil business to the Standard Oil Company, making a huge profit. However, his first love remained the dirtier side of business.

When Storyville opened, Tom was labeled the "Mayor of Storyville." His saloon, located on the corner of Bienville and Basin, was called the gateway to Storyville. His was the first bar in America to be illuminated with electric lights. The bar had one hundred light bulbs in the ceiling, plus an electric-lighted sign outside. The night Tom Anderson opened the bar for business he served one hundred cases of champagne, plus untold cases and barrels of wine, beer, scotch, bourbon, rye, etc., etc. In time, the Anderson bar was the official meeting place of all important gatherings, as well as the unofficial meeting place for the city council.

Anderson was without question the law of all of Storyville. All disputes in the district were heard and ruled upon by him. He was known to be fair, and his word was final. Over the years anybody who was somebody in the United States and visited New Orleans wound up at Anderson's bar in Storyville. P. T. Barnum, Babe Ruth, Diamond Jim Brady, and Ty Cobb were just a few of the hundreds of American notables who partook of Tom's hospitality. Tom had such a high profile in Storyville that many referred to the area as "Anderson Country."

Blue Book

When it came to making a buck, Tom took a back seat to no one. Storyville was a very popular place. Visitors from all over the U. S. and other parts of the world came to New Orleans to visit the popular "red-light district," or as some

Blue Book

PREFACE

"Honi Soit Qui Mal y Pense"

THIS Directory and Guide of the Sporting District has been before the people on many occasions, and has proven its authority to what is doing in the "Queer Zone."

Everybody who knows to-day from yesterday will say that the Blue Book is the right book for the right people.

WHY NEW ORLEANS SHOULD HAVE THIS DIRECTORY

First—Because it is the only district of its kind in the States set aside for the fast women by law.

Second—Because it puts the stranger on a proper and safe path as to where he may go and be free from "Hold-ups," and any other game usually practiced upon the stranger.

Third—It regulates the women so that they may live in one district to themselves instead of being scattered over the city.

LETTER "H" (WHITE)—Continued

Howard, Olga	226 N. Villere
Howard, May	228 N. Villere
Hanford, Annie	429 Marais
HARTMANN, MAUD	327 N. Franklin
Howard, Mildred	327 N. Franklin
Hayes, Ada	337 N. Basin
Howard, Bell	337 N. Basin
Holland, Harriett	225 N. Basin
Hermann, May	315 N. Franklin
Isner, Salra	1424 Customhouse

LETTER "J" (WHITE)

Jantile, Blanche	1128 Customhouse
Jones, Lillie	1419 Customhouse
Jones, Bessie	1320 Conti
Johnson, Florence	1528 Conti
Jones, Elizabeth	1558 Conti
Jones, Louisa	307 N. Villere
Jacobs, Carrie	210 N. Marais
JOHNSON, EMMA	331-33 N. Basin

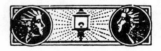

LETTER "W" (COLORED)—Continued

Wilson, Mary	1527 Bienville
Williams, Louise	1518 Bienville
Ward, Ella	1548 Bienville
Williams, Alertha	1548 Bienville
Williams, Cora	1543 Bienville
Webster, Annie	1424 Conti
Withfield, Lottie	1509 Conti
Williams, Sarah	1549 Conti
Williams, Stella	1569 Conti
Wong, Juanita	314 N. Robertson
Webb, Albertha	212 N. Liberty
Walter, Louisa	216 N. Basin

OCTOROONS

WHITE, LULU	235 N. Basin
PIAZZA, WILLIE	315 N. Basin

THIS BOOK MUST NOT BE MAILED

To know the right from the wrong, to be sure of yourself, go through this little book and read it carefully, and then when you visit Storyville you will know the best places to spend your money and time, as all the BEST houses are advertised. Read all the "ads."

The book contains nothing but Facts, and is of the greatest value to strangers when in this part of the city. The Directory will be found alphabetically, under the headings "White" and "Colored," from alpha to omega. The names in capitals are landladies only.

You will find the boundary of the Tenderloin District, or Storyville: North side Iberville Street to south side St. Louis, and east side North Basin to west side North Robertson Streets.

This is the boundary in which the women are compelled to live according to law.

Miss Lulu White

A MAGNIFICENT dark woman, above the ordinary size, with all her massive charms in proportion. She is of a very libidinous disposition, as the brown half-moons beneath her bright eyes can testify. Many are the pranks she has played with her own sex in bed, where she is as lascivious as a goat, but her tastes in that direction do not represent a scandalous itching for the male sex. The man she most cares for is one who can boast of superior size and strength in the part that most delights the weaker sex. In short, this mature lady of about twenty-seven years of age is a most juicy piece, and her appearance always sends an erotic thrill through the habitue. She is about the only woman we have ever met with who could exercise affection for both sexes at one and the same time. She often Sappho by day and Messalina by night, rushing eagerly to the arms of her masculine adorer with the glorious traces of some girlish victim's excitement fresh on her feverish ruby lips.

235 N. Basin

Marguerite and Diana

Why visit the playhouses to see the famous Parisian models portrayed, when one can see the French damsels, Marguerite and Diana? Their names have become known on both continents, because everything goes as it will, and those that cannot be satisfied there must surely be of a queer nature.

They are also known for their singing and dancing.

Don't fail to see these French models in their many poses.

213-215 N. Basin

called it, the "tenderloin district." Because of the high popularity, Tom decided to print and publish a directory.

To head off competition, he owned all or part of five different directories. They were the *Lid, Hello, Sporting Guide, Red Book*, and the *Blue Book*. The *Blue Book* was by far the number one guide to Storyville. Of course, he owned all of that directory. The building where it was printed is still standing.

Tom was a truly amazing man. He is credited with being the first in the world to publish, print, and distribute a directory of prostitutes. Through the years, there were five different categories used when listing the women. They were

W.	White
B.	Black
Q.	Quadroon
O.	Octoroon
*.	Jewish

The names of the madams were listed in bold letters, the working girls in small type. The books sold at railroad stations, steamboat landings, hotels, bars, and restaurants. Where the percentages of clientele who came to Storyville were the highest, Tom made sure that the books were given away free. Local businesses took out ads; for example, Ozone Water, Falstaff Beer, Loubat Restaurant Supplies, etc. Madams also took out colorful ads (see page 226 for examples).

Prostitutes' Mardi Gras Ball

The largest volume of business in Storyville was during Carnival season and Mardi Gras. With his close friend and business associate Jake Lamothe, Tom decided at a meeting at the Anderson Bar that Storyville should be an active participant in the popular and financially-lucrative celebration. It was agreed a prostitutes' Mardi Gras ball would be a huge attraction. Ads were placed in the *Blue Book*

billing the event as the "Ball of the Two Well-Known Gentlemen."

The ball was scheduled to be held at, of all places, Odd Fellows Hall (see page 226). All the madams and girls were excited and anxious to participate. The first ball was, as expected, a huge success. It was far more successful than even Anderson or Lamothe dreamed.

As time went on, the ball got bigger and bigger and drew people from all over the world. Prominent ladies of the city, not of the Storyville profession, wishing to see the event firsthand, had friends get them invitations so they could attend. They had it all figured out. When they went into the ball they would be masked and nobody would know who they were. Word of the plan leaked out. When the madams got wind of the planned intrusion, they made up a counterplan of their own.

On the evening of the ball, after everyone entered, the

madams had friends in high places in the police department raid the ball. All females who could not prove they
were prostitutes were handcuffed, put into paddy wagons,
and taken to the police station, where they were fin-
gerprinted and released. The tactic was highly successful.
The embarrassment suffered by the good society ladies of
New Orleans eliminated any further intrusion into the
Prostitutes' Mardi Gras Ball.

In his golden years, Tom turned 180 degrees, just as
many of the prostitutes of his time did. After becoming
seriously ill, he found religion. He went to church often
and made large contributions to the church and numerous
charities.

On December 10, 1931, at age seventy-three, colorful
and controversial Tom Anderson died. Local newspapers
printed virtually nothing of his rocky past or shady deal-
ings. Instead, they told of his devotion to the church and
his unequalled popularity. They allowed the onetime con-
ductor of organized vice to leave this earth in peace. Who
knows, possibly some of his wealth was used to accentuate
the positive and eliminate the negative. He was able to buy
everything he wanted in life; why not after his death?

Miss Josephine Icebox

Many years before the National Football League's
Chicago Bears' William Perry received the nickname "The
Refrigerator," New Orleans had an equally colorful and
popular character whose nickname was "Josephine Icebox."

"The Refrigerator," playing a contact sport with great
emotion, received his nickname because of his immense
size. The diminutive-framed Josephine Clare, on the other
hand, got hers because of her lack of emotion in her
chosen profession, which could also be classified as a contact sport. Josephine was the prime attraction at Madam
Gertie Livingston's establishment in the infamous "red-

MISS JOSEPHINE ICEBOX

light district" in New Orleans. Gertie, better known to the
sporting crowd as "Her Majesty, Queen Gertie," advertised
various prizes for any patron who could defrost Josephine,
who Gertie claimed was the most "frigid tart" in the district. So far as it is known, the widely known and im-
mensely popular "Josephine Icebox" was never defrosted.

Josie Arlington

Born Mary Deubler in 1864, she had an Irish father who
was very, very strict. At the age of seventeen, Mary came
home from a date later than her father told her she could.
Because of her disobedience, he turned her away.

Miss Josie Arlington

THE ARLINGTON

NOWHERE IN
this country
will you find a
more complete
and thorough
sporting house
than the
ARLINGTON
Absolutely
and unques-
tionably the
most decorat-
ive and costly
fitted out sport-
ing palace ever
placed before
the American
public.
The wonder-
ful originality
of everything
that goes to fit
out a mansion
makes it the
most attract-
ive ever seen
in this or the
old country.
Miss Arlington, after suffering a
loss of many thousand dollars
through a fire, has refurnished and
remodeled the entire place at an
enormous expense, and the mansion is now a palace fit for a king.
Within the great walls of this
mansion will be found the work of
great artists from Europe and America. Many articles from various ex-
positions will also be seen, and cu-
rios galore.

PHONE MAIN 1888

225 N. Basin

Mary's boyfriend, Philip Lobrano, a real nice guy, found employment for her working in one of the many houses of ill repute of the day. Philip also gave her a new name—Josie Alton. She worked hard and supported not only Philip, but several members of her family. Philip did not like the idea. He called these members of her family vultures. In time he shot and killed Mary's brother. The court set him free and so did Mary.

It was said that Josie Alton was hell on wheels. She was constantly in fights. In one brawl, she bit off half of an ear and a good part of the lower lip of Beulah Ripley, an unliked competitor. Josie gained the reputation of being this city's toughest harlot. This was quite an achievement when you consider the competition.

For unknown reasons, out of the blue one day, Josie decided to turn over a new leaf. First, she changed her name to d'Arlington, and shortly thereafter to Josie Arlington. Her new policy as a madam was to hire only "amiable foreign girls" and cater to only refined gentlemen. The Arlington House, as advertised in the *Blue Book*, was a four-story Edwardian building topped with a Neo-Byzantine Cupola. It was further stated that the wonderful originality of its furnishings made it the most attractive mansion ever seen in this or the old country.

The building featured Turkish, Japanese, Viennese, and American parlors. The house was furnished with pile oriental rugs, life-like paintings and sculptures, and many of the items from the 1884 New Orleans World's Fair. There were paintings by great European artists, sculptures from around the world, and the *Blue Book* noted that there was musical entertainment at the Arlington at all times.

The Arlington was located at 225 N. Basin Street. Although Josie advertised "all foreign girls," this was an untruth. LaBelle Stewart was advertised as a bona fide baroness from the court of St. Petersburg. In truth, she was a hoochy-koochy dancer from the midway of the Chicago

World's Fair. Another girl supposedly from the Russian court was a circus specialist. The patrons didn't seem to mind, though. They packed the house on a regular basis.

One night, the Arlington suffered a severe fire. Josie came close to losing her life. She lived, but the traumatic experience affected her mind. She purchased and moved into a palatial home on Esplanade Avenue. She bought an expensive plot in Metairie Cemetery, then ordered a huge red marble tomb. The tomb has a cross on the back and a large copper door on the front. Placed at the front door of the tomb was a beautiful statue of a young girl, around seventeen years of age, knocking at the door of the tomb.

There are two stories regarding this statue. One is that it symbolizes Mary knocking at her door and being turned away by her father. The second is that it is a reminder of Josie's boast that she never allowed a virgin to work in her establishment; this statement, according to her competitors, was untrue.

Upon her death, Josie was buried in the beautiful red tomb. Unfortunately for her, the city installed a traffic light on the street behind her tomb. The red light reflected on the red marble. Word got out that even though Josie was gone her tomb was still in a red-light district. Crowds of people swarmed to see this oddity. Someone added to the already crowded and congested condition around her tomb by placing a red lantern in the hand of the statue at the front of her tomb. The tomb was ultimately sold and Josie's remains were moved to an unknown final resting place.

See page 231 for a copy of Josie's ad in the *Blue Book*.

Lulu White—More Glitter than the St. Louis Exposition

In the 1880s, a short, fat, unattractive female octoroon with a masculine voice arrived in the Crescent City from

Selma, Alabama. Her name was Lulu White. It wasn't long before her name was on the police blotter at frequent intervals, the day she arrived being the first. In her years in the city, she was arrested for prostitution, disturbing the peace, and white slavery, to mention just a few of her indiscretions.

What Lulu lacked in looks she made up for in showmanship and good business sense. She went the usual route working for others, but only until she could survey the situation. It didn't take long for her to get the financial backing of and the all-important contacts with not one, but three very important businessmen. She had a special talent in this area, for it was said whatever she wanted financially she received.

Her one weakness was her pimp, George Killshaw. He was slim, good-looking, well-dressed, and his charm melted Lulu's heart. Yes, George was as slippery as an Exxon oil slick. He handled her as easily as she handled others.

Lulu's place in Storyville was called Mahogany Hall. With the open-pocketbook assistance she received, it was either grand or gaudy, depending on your taste. The four-story palace, as Lulu referred to it, was staffed with beautiful octoroon women. Mahogany Hall ads boasted of the hall of mirrors that cost over $30,000. The massive parlors had huge cut-glass mirrors everywhere. Each bedroom was also furnished with mirrors on the ceilings and at the head and foot of each bed. From the ceilings throughout the house hung cut-glass chandeliers, each costing, as pointed out in her ads, a small fortune.

Patrons, upon arriving at Mahogany Hall, were cordially welcomed by General Jack Johnson. He wore a pure white, wrinkle-free uniform. General Jack was a forty-inch-tall black midget doorman whose smile was as wide as his height. From there, the patrons entered the hall of mirrors, where they were greeted by evening-gowned beauties. Lulu hired only well-known and respected musicians to entertain her guests. Jelly Roll Morton, Clarence Williams, and Kidd Ross all worked for Lulu at various times.

One of the highlights of the evening was Lulu's entrance. When she descended the marble stairway with her long evening dress swirling and her fire-red hair (wig) glistening in the light, she drew the attention of everyone. Her smile was only quickly glanced at, for patrons quickly turned their attention to her diamond-studded tiara, massive diamond necklace, diamond earrings costing $7,400,

diamond bracelets on both arms, and diamond rings on each and every finger, including her thumbs.

It is said Lulu would wear jewelry wherever it would fit. Yes, she was, as advertised, more sparkling than the St. Louis Exposition. The display of brilliant diamonds distracted attention from her lack of beauty.

Lulu had her own promotional booklet similar to the *Blue Book*. She opted, because she recognized that she was not a beauty, to use the photo of one of the beautiful girls who worked for her. The patrons did not seem to mind.

Lulu enjoyed tremendous financial success in her field. The one place she did not succeed was with George Killshaw. Lulu made a trip to Hollywood, where she spoke to the people in the movie industry about starting her own movie studio. With all of the ground work laid, Lulu returned to New Orleans. When everything was ready, and the business deal was ready to be consummated, she was just too busy to go back to California, so she sent George with $150,000 in cash to close the deal. George took the money and was never heard from again. Lulu must have thought, "easy come, easy go." She loved George even after he ran off with the $150,000. She did not even bother to have anyone look for him or the money. She was sure he would return on his own one day.

In her lifetime, Lulu made a vast fortune. Yet when she died, she was penniless. Not even George Killshaw came to her rescue after her death. She was ultimately buried in Potters Field.

Although Lulu may have died a pauper, her lifestyle, especially the flashy part, was reenacted by Mae West in the movie *The Belle of The 90s*. The part played by Mae West was lived by Lulu White here in New Orleans.

Lulu was unquestionably a multi-talented person. Further proof of this can be read in Lulu White's ad in the *Blue Book* on page 226.

Emma Johnson

If you had to select one madam who was the most depraved and totally devoid of feelings or human emotions of any kind, who would literally do anything for profit in full view of a crowd, it was Emma Johnson. Her establishment was located at 331–335 Basin Street, and was the largest building in the district. In this hellhole could be found a huge theatre/ballroom where her "circuses" were held.

Emma was drawn to lesbianism early in her life. It was said she had the capacity to get an unbelievable hold on many of her own sex. Those of the female sex who did not commit to her uncanny ability were drugged into doing her will. She had a psychotic tendency for exhibitionism. Knowing she could earn more performing for a large group than for a single person, she arranged and engaged in performances of sadomasochism, fetishism, and voyeurism, to mention just a few.

When Storyville officially closed in 1917, Emma's circuses were still very popular, with standing room only at every performance. Even though she was then close to sixty years of age, she was still performing to the delight of the crowds. In spite of being a repeated violator of many laws, with overwhelming evidence against her, she was never convicted of anything. She never spent one day in jail or paid one dollar in fines. It was believed the reason for this injustice was that the city fathers knew that her establishment was one of the main attractions for convention managers who selected New Orleans.

Cawzi

In the history of Storyville, only one man performed regularly there; this does not include musicians, bartenders, doormen, etc. His name was Cawzi. In spite of his slim, frail look, he participated in the circuses in ten performances a week for twelve consecutive years. He received $150 per week for his services, which enabled him to send all of his children to college. He was labeled one of the unbelievable "wonders of the district." As he so ably phrased it, he may have looked frail, but he was well endowed where it counted, and equally endowed with the stamina necessary for the show.

Cawzi was also an entrepreneur. Based on his highly energetic performance at the circus, he sold his own form of pep pills. He had no trouble selling to the majority of the men who attended and witnessed his performance in the circus. He did have trouble with government authorities who warned him to discontinue selling the pills or he would go to jail.

Cawzi was alive and well in the late half of the 1970s. He claimed at that time that he was still man enough to play the role he performed at Emma's circus.

THE END OF STORYVILLE

In August of 1917, by order of U.S. Secretary of War Newton D. Baker and Secretary of the Navy Josephus

Daniels, open prostitution was banned within five miles of any U.S. Army installation. Mr. Bascom Johnson, representing the War and Navy departments, visited Storyville and interviewed some of the leaders of the district. He declared the area was within five miles of an army base, and advised Mayor Martin Behrman to close it down.

On September 10, the mayor traveled to Washington to plead his case. All doors were tightly closed to him. On September 24, Behrman received an illegal threat to close down Storyville or the armed forces would. With no other recourse, Behrman presented to the city council an ordinance providing for the official closing of Storyville. On October 9, under protest, the council passed the ordinance, with the official closing date set for November 12, 1917. On this day, the only legal red-light district in the U.S. came to an abrupt end.

WHAT WE LEARNED FROM STORYVILLE

When Storyville opened in 1897, 2,000 prostitutes occupied 230 houses. When it closed in 1917, there were less than 400 women still working, with half only working part-time. Within a year, venereal diseases were back because prostitutes were no longer required to obtain regular medical checkups, crimes against nature jumped up, unwed mothers were on the rise, and houses of ill repute sprang up all over town, including in the French Quarter and the elaborate Garden District.

In time, even the street walkers were out in force. Police books again became filled with ineffectual arrests. Payoffs to politicians and policemen again assumed major proportions. Bellboys who worked in the better hotels were paying $1,000 per year for their positions because of the money they could make pimping.

In spite of what Storyville had done to eliminate the monumental problems the city faced prior to Storyville, when it did close down efforts were made by those opposed to it to do everything in their power to make people think it never existed. The *Times-Picayune* newspaper threw out its files of photos of Storyville. The library suppressed information on Storyville. Articles in newspapers and periodicals were cut out. The name of Basin Street was changed to N. Saratoga, but later changed back. The crowning blow was that almost all the buildings of Storyville were torn down, and a housing project was put in its place.

The story of Storyville is a good example of the old saying, "The one thing we learn from history is that for the most part we don't learn anything from history."